the Smart Approach to the organized home

THE AGENCY
TOM WOLFE
GREG ILES
INDIAN KILLER

the Smart Approach to the organized home

Leslie Plummer Clagett

CREATIVE HOMEOWNER®, Upper Saddle River, New Jersey

CREATIVE
HOMEOWNER®

A Division of Federal Marketing Corp.
Upper Saddle River, NJ

The Smart Approach to® the Organized Home
Senior Editor: Kathie Robitz
Senior Designer: Glee Barre
Contributing Editor: Elaine Petrowski
Layout Artist: Diane P. Smith-Gale
Editorial Assistants: Evan Lambert (proofreading);
Lauren Manoy and Robyn Poplasky (photo research)
Indexer: Schroeder Indexing Services
Cover Design: Glee Barre
Front Cover Photography: Brian Vanden Brink
Inside Front Cover Photography: (top) Alan Shortall;
(bottom) Brian Vanden Brink
Back Cover Photography: (top left) Alan Shortall;
(bottom left) Niall McDiarmid/Redcover.com;
(right) courtesy of Ikea
Inside Back Cover Photography: (top) Alan Shortall;
(bottom) Ed Reeve/Redcover.com

Creative Homeowner
VP/Publisher: Brian Toolan
VP/Editorial Director: Timothy O. Bakke
Production Manager: Kimberly H. Vivas
Art Director: David Geer
Managing Editor: Fran Donegan

The Smart Approach to® the Organized Home, First Edition
Library of Congress Control Number: 2005924460
ISBN-10: 1-58011-252-8
ISBN-13: 978-1-58011-252-9

Current Printing (last digit)
10 9 8 7 6 5 4 3 2
Printed in China

CREATIVE HOMEOWNER®
A Division of Federal Marketing Corp.
24 Park Way
Upper Saddle River, NJ 07458
www.creativehomeowner.com

ACKNOWLEDGMENTS

I'd like to extend my sincere appreciation to the capable team at Creative Homeowner, foremost Kathie Robitz, Elaine Petrowski, and Diane Smith. Their professionalism wholly brought this book to life.

For his unflagging support throughout projects literary and otherwise, I thank my husband, John.

CONTENTS

INTRODUCTION

Whether you're just stumped for ways to gain space, or you urgently need to stem the tide of stuff that's rapidly filling the house from basement to attic to garage, *The Smart Approach to the Organized Home* can help you define and achieve your organizational and living goals in a smart and stylish fashion. Developing and putting into practice a successful storage strategy isn't just about maintaining a veneer of neatness, nor is it a rote pursuit for compulsive personalities. The true effect of storage is actually intangible; it preserves the particular quality of life in every room of your home. And so, this book examines the home room-by-room—entryways to kitchens, attics to garages—and provides both general guidelines as well as loads of specific examples of storage ideas that are both informative and inspiring.

Starting with Chapter 1, "Ready, Set, Get Organized," pages 12-21, you'll find a master plan for how and where to begin your own campaign against clutter. You'll discover exactly what special kind of storage is right for your particular situation. You'll weigh the pros and cons of built-in solutions versus add-on or retrofit fixes, and outline methods for keeping your organizational program on track.

In Chapter 2, "Front Entries and Mudrooms," pages 22-31, you'll find ideas for crafting a welcoming space both just outside the door and over the threshold. You'll also learn how to create an appealing transition from the outdoors into your home. The second half of the chapter focuses on the mudroom. Completely informal in style and wonderfully practical, this old-fashioned space is popular again.

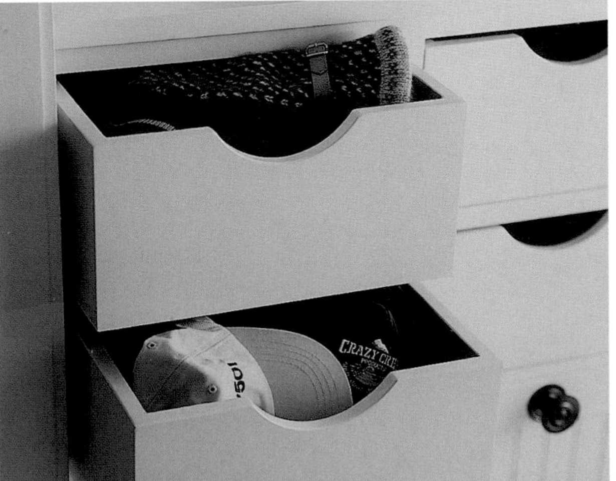

Chapter 3, "Ideas for the Kitchen," pages 32-49, deals with reclaiming the countertop, organizing the drawers, and maximizing the cabinet spaces in ways that respond to how you use the room.

Chapter 4, "Living and Family Rooms," pages 50-69, focuses on two important public areas of your home: the living and family rooms. Will they show off your style sense or expose you as a perennial pack rat? The right furniture, artful display, and thoughtful storage play a key role, as you'll see in these pages.

Whether it's a dedicated room for sit-down dinners or a room that serves multiple functions, the dining room will always be ready for spontaneous meals or special occasions if you follow the good advice offered in Chapter 5, "Dining Room Gatherings," pages 70-83.

Sweet dreams or your worst nightmare—which one describes the bedroom in your home? In chapter 6, "Rethinking Bedroom Storage," pages 84-107, learn how to tame all kinds of clutter—under the bed, on the floor, and in the closet.

Chapter 7, "Organizing the Bathroom," pages 108-123, focuses on the bath: home to medicines and Mr. Bubble. You'll find multiple solutions for all types of bathrooms.

What's the difference between a rec room and a wrecked room? Find out in Chapter 8, "Relaxing at Home," pages 124-137, which discusses organization in the media room and library.

Chapter 9, "The Home Office," pages 138-157, fills the bill if you're intimidated by the state of your desk and beyond. Here's how to organize everything—even all that paper.

Chapter 10, "Attics, Basements & Laundries," pages 158-177, outlines what should—and shouldn't—be exposed to these often hot or damp areas, and the best ways to protect your belongings.

Chapter 11, "Garage, Shops & Crafts Areas," pages 178–187, takes the mystery out of organizing tools and materials for hobbies that can be as varied as scrapbooking and woodworking.

Chapter 12, "Outdoor Spaces," pages 188–197, helps you get control of your outdoor storage needs with ideas that put hazardous pool, barbecue, and gardening equipment under secure wraps.

Left: Become the envy of your friends: a custom walk-in closet and dressing room is today's status symbol.

Opposite: Moving the office into the home calls for storage that is functional yet has flair.

The Ultimate Rose Book
WELLER POTTERY

EXIT
ALLENKNIT SWIM SUITS
ON THE CREST OF THE ST
Allen A
GONE
BOATING

CHAPTER 1

READY, SET, GET ORGANIZED

- A PLAN OF ACTION
- ROOM TO BUILD

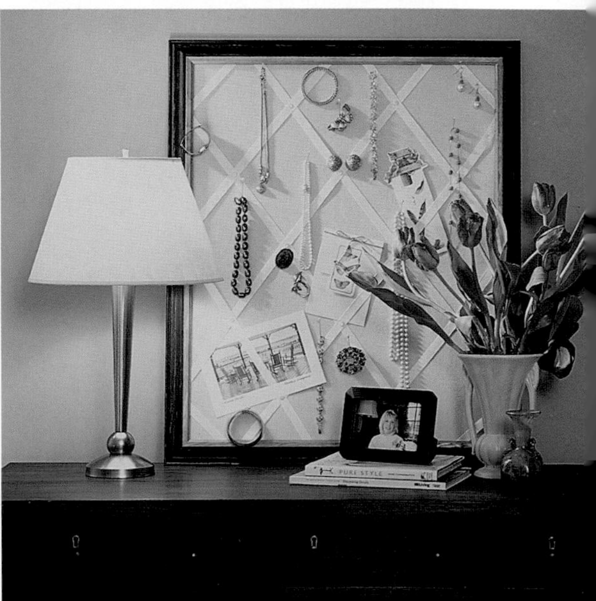

The car keys were last seen in the upstairs bedroom—or were they on the table in the family room? Your partner can't find the tools he needs to get going on that weekend project. It seems your 3-year-old is missing half the pieces to his favorite puzzle, again. And even though you've been on the hunt for the checkbook (you know you saw it "somewhere" recently), it hasn't turned up yet.

If this is what some days are like at your house, you need "a place for your stuff," says comedian George Carlin. "That's all your house is: a place to keep your stuff. If you didn't have so much stuff, you wouldn't need a house. You could just walk around all the time." Well, not exactly, but he's got a point: "stuff," or too much of it, can complicate your life. Although you may think you and the other members of your household are too busy to clear out and tidy up regularly, the fact is, getting the place organized will ultimately save time. Less clutter means fewer frantic searches for what you need, when you need it. Being organized means you can find that tool for the next task exactly where you left it, in its appointed place. And fewer harried hunts lead to calmer days and a more peaceful home environment. In this chapter, you'll find some general ideas for eliminating clutter—once and for all!

A PLAN OF ACTION

Become disciplined with your time. Form a routine for picking up and putting away important items, and throwing out what you don't need. Don't wait for spring or fall to take stock of the entire household. It's a year-round, ongoing process. Depending on your schedule, try to keep up with small projects on a weekly basis; another approach is to devote 15 minutes a day to these tasks. You'll learn that getting (and staying) organized is easier than you think, once you get the system down. Being "the organized type" is not a genetic trait, even if it seems to come naturally to others. However, it can be habit-forming: learn it and pass it on to your kids. The best part is that once you do get the basic techniques down and develop some organizational skills you'll be able to apply them to all aspects of your life, from the front door to the attic rafters and all the shelves, pantries, nooks, crannies, closets, and drawers in between.

TAKING A HOME INVENTORY

Before choosing a storage system, you have to think about the types of things that need to be organized. Start counting: multiples of the same type of things, such as clothing, for example, should be kept in the same place but separated according to type (sizes, seasonal, evening wear, and so forth). Objects for display are another story. Measure each one (noting the height and width) so that you can select an appropriately scaled cabinet and shelves for the collection.

Are you looking for a way to store items that are very similar in form? If that's the case, you're in luck. Things such as bottles of wine, shoes, DVDs, and dinner plates are examples of objects that, because of their uniformity and standard sizes, are quite easy to organize using off-the-shelf accessories or the most basic built-in designs

Above: Reserve open storage, particularly in the kitchen, for items you use—and wash—regularly.

Left: Vary drawer capacities so that you can store and easily get access to items of different sizes.

SMARTtip Take Small Bites

Organizing an entire house can be a daunting task. Learn from what the pros know and take it one small step at a time. Target one room; within that room target one area; in that area, target one spot—a closet, a drawer, or a corner.

Perhaps in another part of the house you're confronting a hodgepodge of articles of all sizes and shapes. Think of the variety of tools in a workshop, all the gear and gadgets in your kitchen, the kids' sports equipment, or crafts materials. Recognizing that you need to find a place for long rolls of wrapping paper, softball-sized balls of twine, sheets of labels, postage stamps, and stickers in the same area is half the battle.

Quantity. Is there a fixed number of articles to be stored, or will the collection expand and contract? Being able to anticipate the amount of storage needed over time means you won't outgrow the capacity of your storage system quite as fast (if at all). For example, if you buy staples and sundries in bulk at the discount store, you probably have a good idea of just how much of these items you normally have on hand—there's never less than a case of soda in the pantry, but never more than three cases, for example. Book-club members can count on accommodating at least 12 new volumes a year on their shelves. It's harder to anticipate the long-range needs of a new baby who's on the way or a child who's off to college.

Above: Rollouts make it easy to retrieve the items at the back of a drawer or tray.

Above Right: Use every inch: bottle storage found a place at the end of a cabinet run here.

Right: Vary shelf heights to suit the size and number of items you plan to store.

"Stuff" Happens—The Five Life Stages

You know something's got to be done—but how did it come to this? For many people, the genesis and evolution of personal clutter goes like this:

1. **Mess? What Mess? (ages 1-4):** Standard procedure is to throw everything—clothes, food, toys—on the floor. No need to worry; someone else will pick it all up and put it away. Life is good.
2. **The Show-off Stage (ages 5-10):** Here's when you find out if the hoarding gene is a dominant or recessive trait in your family. Acquisitiveness trumps organizational skills for these years, during which "my" collection of Barbie dolls, Beanie Babies, or Hot Wheels is always bigger (and better) than yours. Display, while it could hardly be viewed as artistically executed, starts to become a paramount concern.
3. **Don't Touch My Stuff (ages 11-16):** Issues of ownership and territoriality arise, and abruptly so. The result, as seen in such innocent incursions as collecting laundry from a teen's room, is a highly personal, borderline paranoid approach to organization. But don't fret—it's only a phase (albeit a rather rigid one). Then one day it suddenly gives way to its near-polar opposite. Crazy.
4. **Sure. Whatever (ages 17-21):** Organization is most assuredly off the radar screen, as young adults are more focused on social interaction than a well-planned storage system—at least for the time being. Thanks to the ubiquitous plastic milk-carton crate used as a catchall for everything from books to stereos to T-shirts, dorm rooms around the world are saved from total chaos.
5. **Help! (currently in progress):** Symptoms include a to-do list that never gets shorter, perpetually nagging family members to "pick that up, put that away," and frustration engendered by never finding the right time—or any time at all—to tackle the ever-expanding situation. Where should you start? Congratulations. If you're reading this, at least you recognize that there's a problem.

Size and Shape. The best way to get a handle on the physical requirements of storage is to measure the elements involved. Whether it's linear feet of books, the lengths of rakes and shovels, or the depth of a television set, knowing all the dimensions of the items to be stored will be the linchpin of the solution. Keep a tape measure on hand as you organize your spaces. The consequences of not measuring are straightforward: if something won't fit into its new home, chances are good that it won't get put away at all. Making the extra effort to plan your storage conscientiously means you won't fall into this self-defeating trap.

ACCESSIBILITY

Children and able adults have different capabilities, as do elderly people and those with physical limitations. Who uses the items in question?

Analyzing this situation from a storage point of view can often shed light on the solution. For instance, drawers are easier to access, both on a physical and visual basis,

Below: Make it easy to be neat. Accessible storage is more likely to be used consistently by all family members.

for many seniors and kids than are shelves and cabinets. A row of pegs or hooks installed on a wall at the right height for the user increases the likelihood that items will be put away regularly.

Frequency. How frequently do you use specific items? Several times a day? Weekly? On a seasonal basis—or maybe even only a couple times a year? A basic premise of effective storage is the more often something is used, the more accessible it should be. An example: put the seasonings you use frequently in the front row of the spice rack, leaving the back row for things you use only occasionally. And don't put Valentine's Day stuff into the linen closet, where it will idly occupy valuable space that could be put to better use.

Location. Where are things needed? Storage professionals make a strong case for keeping articles close to their point of first or last usage. This strategy saves both steps and time. It makes sense to keep seasonings and spices near the range, as it does to stash utensils in a crock on the countertop. Hobby materials don't belong in the living room if you work on your crafts projects in the dining room. Why struggle to drag outdoor furniture into the basement, when keeping it in the garage would be more convenient?

Ergonomics, the study of interactive human engineering, dictates some locations. Particularly in the cabinetry-rich kitchen, but elsewhere in the home, too, ergonomics mandates some storage principles relative to both where items are stowed and when they're used. For example, frequently used items are best placed within an arm's reach, approximately between hip- and eye-level. Objects that are needed slightly less often can be placed just beyond this zone, where either crouching or stretching will put them within your grasp. Articles that see rare usage can be stashed away in spots where they can be reached with the help of a step stool.

Specialized Storage. Finally, take stock of any special qualities the articles may have. Knowing the nature of what will be squirreled away can help determine not only how to store something but also where it should go. Are the items

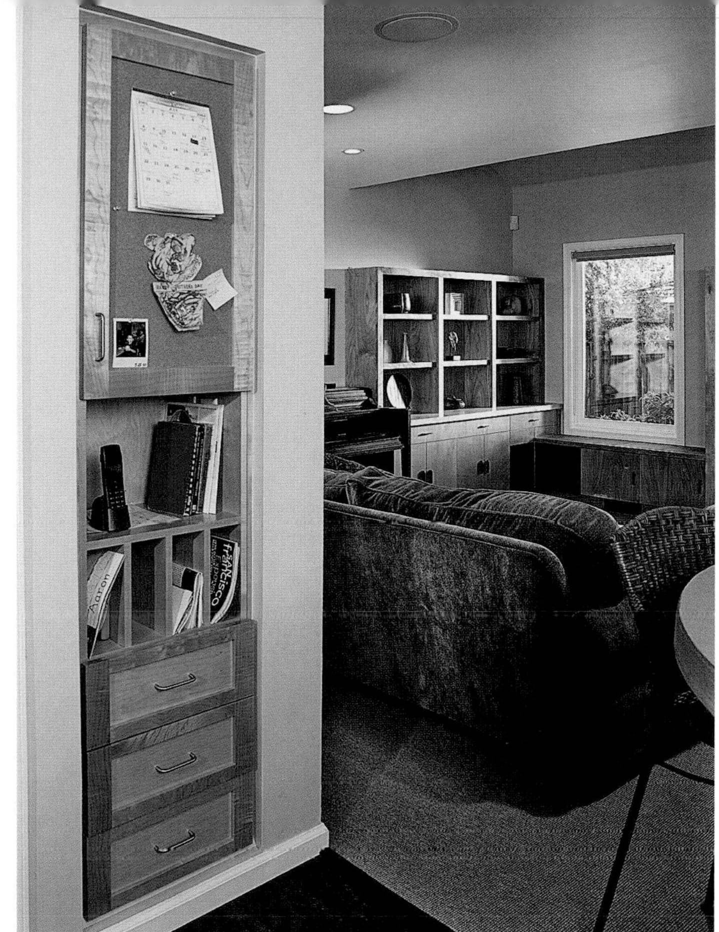

Above: Organize a message center in a central gathering space such as the kitchen or family room.

Below: Brighten a hardworking home office by including space for favorite collectibles.

Left: Platters stay neat on slide-out shelves designed to store each one separately. Ironed tablecloths remain wrinkle-free on padded hangers.

Right: Open shallow shelves fit the bill in a dressing room. Items are easy to see but neatly tucked away. A tied-back curtain adds a decorative touch.

Below: You can attractively mix display and accessible storage.

delicate—such as fabric, photography, or personal mementos, which are all sensitive to light, moisture, or temperature? Wrapping fabrics in sheets of acid-free tissue before boxing them up gently insulates them as well as protects against dust and creasing. Keep things such as photos, paper mementos, important documents, and books out of the damp cellar, grimy garage, or uncontrolled climate extremes of the attic.

Security. Do any of the items require high-security storage? Chemicals and medications should be off-limits to anyone except their rightful, responsible users; a lockable cabinet is a must. For irreplaceable documents or data, consider a safe or a fireproof file box, at least.

If you don't feel qualified to determine what to do with something of value, consult a professional.

STORAGE CATEGORIES

When it comes to deciding where to put certain objects, there are three main categories from which to choose: display, accessible but concealed, and deep storage. Each serves a distinct and separate need.

On Display. The most purely aesthetic form of storage, display space provides you with a way to attractively organize many items so they're out of the way but always visible. Examples of household display include a wall in the entryway that's filled with framed photographs, tabletop arrangements of heirloom trinket boxes in the den, or a collection of vintage salt and pepper shakers in a glass-fronted kitchen cabinet. With the exception of utility areas, such as the basement, garage, and attic, well-planned displays can integrate decor with organization throughout the home.

Ready to Use. Close at hand yet out of sight: that's the definition of accessible concealed storage. As many of life's necessities aren't inherently handsome, this variety of storage has lots of potential applications in just about every room of the house. Toiletries in the bathroom, cleaning supplies in the kitchen, socks and underwear in the bedroom—all can benefit from organization.

Out of Sight. Deep storage is the organizational equivalent of the out-of-sight, out-of-mind perspective. This is reserved for articles that don't see constant or even regular use, such as holiday decorations, luggage, seasonal sports equipment, and depending on where you live, perhaps patio furniture and pool accessories. Locations for this kind of storage are, as you would think, the more remote parts of the house: up in the attic, down in the cellar, or perhaps out in the garage or tool shed.

One Man's Trash

If you decide to hold a yard or garage sale, follow these tried-and-true staging methods:

1. **Set a date.** Don't have a sale on a holiday weekend. Have a fall-back date—and include it in your ads if it looks as if there's a possibility the weather won't cooperate.

2. **Make a marketing plan.** Check out the local newspapers; many of them have classified sections that are devoted to yard sale listings. Pin up notices on bulletin boards. If you're selling anything that might be of interest to collectors or small-business owners, make sure to mention it in your ads and signs. For example: "Nancy Drew: the complete series," "PC software," "baby things." Don't forget directions and sale hours in your ad.

3. **Organize the merchandise.** Put clothing in one area, and subdivide it into men's, women's, and children's garments. (All clothes should be washed before the sale.) Keep all kitchen gadgets, cooking paraphernalia, tools, and accessories close together. Clearly tag all items with their prices using stick-on labels. To save time and effort, gather a single category of goods—say ties, or handbags—put them into a large cardboard box and label it "Everything $3." If you're putting small electric appliances or entertainment equipment on the block, try to have a power outlet accessible so buyers can be assured things are working.

4. **Price to sell.** While you might look forward to reaping a profit from this purge, know that nobody ever got rich from a garage sale. Your objective is to clear out the clutter. Cast a cold, impartial eye on things when placing a value on them. Set prices in rounded amounts of currency—a quarter, dollars—to lessen the likelihood you'll need to make change. And make sure you have some change (coins and smaller bills) in the kitty before you begin. If a buyer offers less than the sticker price, don't waste time haggling; you're not in this for the money, remember? For the last hour of the sale, slash your prices in half, and erect a sign advertising this incentive.

5. **Have an exit strategy, and stick to it.** Let the end of the sale be the end: put everything that's unsold at the close of the day into bags or boxes, and cart them off the premises—not back into the basement. Hold firm, and haul the remaining stuff away to the Goodwill shop. If there are any major appliances or large pieces of furniture left over, a local clean-out service will likely take them off your hands for a modest fee.

SMART tip — Skirt the Issue

Here's one fast way to hide all kinds of stuff: put it in boxes or plastic containers that fit under a table. Use a pretty fabric tablecloth to conceal it.

In some cases, the best answer may involve a combination of more than one kind of storage. For instance, in a kitchen you could show off a collection of copper pots and pans, and still have them convenient to your cooktop. A ceiling-mounted pot rack addresses both those concerns in a blend of display and accessible storage types.

Three steps sum up the preliminary preparations you'll need to do to carry out a thorough home organization.

ONE Prioritize. Why should you waste storage space on worn-out clothing, broken tools, or computer equipment that's so old it's incompatible with the rest of your home office? The time has come to sever the bonds. The first rule for organizing your stuff is to sift through it for what you really do use and need. Hold on to what's useful or truly meaningful; jettison the rest. If you still have trouble deciding what's a keeper, apply this test: anything you or family members haven't put to active use in 18 months should go. Donate serviceable clothing and furniture to a charity, or hold a yard sale. If it's possible, recycle materials. The landfill should be the last resort.

TWO Categorize. Once you've separated the wheat from the chaff, so to speak, group the objects you're going to store or put on display. The best approach is a simple and systematic one: sort by common characteristics such as size, color, or purpose, all while keeping in mind the kind of storage you need.

THREE Organize. Having pared down and sorted out, you're ready to reassemble the parts of your new puzzle. That's where the rest of this book kicks in. As you go forward through each chapter, you'll discover specific solutions to a wide array of storage problems.

ROOM TO BUILD

Think of environments that are entirely self-contained: submarines, motor homes, and sailing ships. These are the ultimate examples of the fascinating possibilities of built-in storage solutions, where each thing truly has its place and every space has a purpose.

Ahh, if only you were drifting in the middle of the Mediterranean Sea, miles from the coast, instead of living just a 20-minute drive from the mecca of material temptation—the mall. Yes, unchecked consumerism is the root of many clutter problems, but there is a positive side of this situation. You're also close to lots of sources for help: the hardware store, specialty home-storage shops, and cabinetmakers—all of these can significantly ease your organizational woes and challenges.

A straightforward accounting of the pros and cons of built-in storage might assist you in deciding whether it's the route for you to take.

In the pros column, there is the fact that custom-built cabinets and closets can be made to fit your home's physical space and sized to your needs. A well-executed job will blend seamlessly into your living space, becoming both an architectural asset and a boost to your home's value.

Opposite bottom: Custom built-ins can be an architectural asset.

Right: An organized home office may help improve your productivity: no time is wasted rummaging for office supplies or that file you need.

Below: A clever design features a custom door unit that has shelves on one side.

On the cons side of the argument, built-ins cost more, sometimes much more, than off-the-shelf storage systems. In addition, you may not be able to adapt a custom unit should your needs change. One more thing: anything that is designed and made from scratch for you will take time to complete.

Accessories offer a quick and easy alternative to built-in solutions. Simple containers are a sure way to bring at least fundamental order to things, although if they're too large the contents can remain a jumble. In that case, include dividers. Plastic or galvanized metal bins keep workshops tidy; hand-woven baskets bring a pleasing neatness to the closet or laundry room; the desk in a home office can be whipped into shape with an array of items, such as vertical files, in- and out-boxes, and a pencil cup.

Then there is a more sophisticated class of add-ons, geared mostly toward stretching the capacity of existing cabinets. These include lazy Susans, rotating tiered inserts, shelf boosters, rolling trays, pullouts, and tilt-out drawers.

THE UNUSUAL SUSPECTS

Surprising opportunities for storage pop up throughout the house: on or inside the walls, under floorboards, inside a stair, hanging from a ceiling, and more. You'll find suggestions for these unexpected prospects throughout the following chapters. Hopefully, you'll soon be able to envision once unimagined possibilities in your own home.

ORGANIZING TOOLS AND HELPERS

As you undertake cleaning out, reorganizing, and then storing the items in a particular room or area, you'll need the following bunch of items on hand. First is a large trash can. If you can't manage that, at least use large sturdy plastic bags for all the items that you'll want to discard. Don't just make another pile on the floor or the bed. Use sturdy cardboard boxes for sorting or categorizing items, labeling them with an indelible marker. Keep a measuring tape nearby for measuring things you'll want to put away and for calculating how much storage capacity a basket, shelf, or closet yields. Don't forget to load up on packing tape and a dispenser, bubble wrap, and tissue or archival paper. Purchase color-coded file folders or loose-leaf binders to keep papers together and neat.

CHAPTER 2

FRONT ENTRIES AND MUDROOMS

- FOYER FINESSE
- MUDROOMS WITHOUT MADNESS

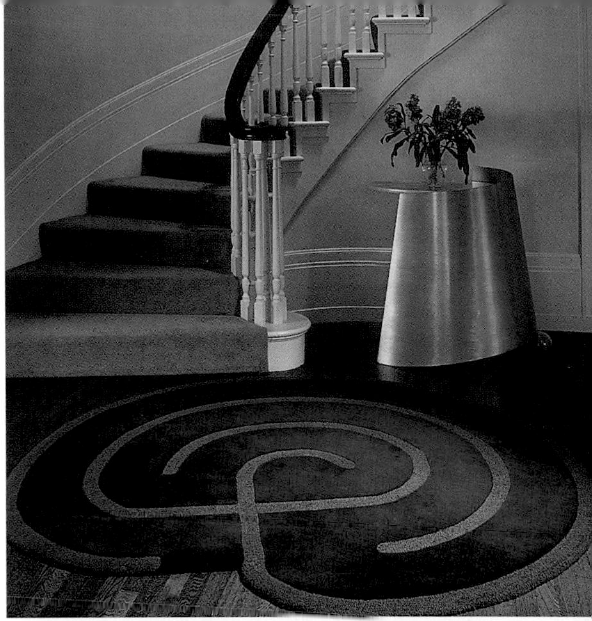

Whether you call it the foyer, vestibule, or entry, the often-small interim space that provides a passage from the street into your home is asked to serve several functions. It's where visitors are greeted and family members are welcomed back into the warmth of home. As the first public space visitors see, the entry provides an initial glimpse into, and therefore the first impression of, your home. If there's a mirror and the right light, it's the place to do a last-minute check of your personal appearance before you open the door.

The front foyer or the back entry is usually the designated place to remove outer gear. And it's always handy if there's room to put down your purse or briefcase. Depending on the layout and whether there's room for a coat rack or closet, there may be a place for guests' coats as well as your own. In a busy household, an entry may offer a convenient spot for the mail, the keys, or someplace to recharge your cell phone. Obviously, this little space is a lot more important than you might have thought.

Entries signal your family's style and energy. If it's one of cluttered chaos right now, it's time to change it through a careful reassessment and reorganization of the space to add flair and make it more functional.

Above: An expanse of glass and warm lighting immediately welcomes guests.

While the storage demands of both front and back entry rooms are basically the same—jackets and coats, umbrellas, mail—and the items need to be easily accessible, the ambiance and overall design of front entryways and back-door mudrooms are far-flung cousins, indeed. Polished and refined, the former welcomes guests on special occasions, while the latter is a utilitarian, everyday portal used by family members. The quality and quantity of storage for each location varies accordingly.

However, a gracious welcome or warm homecoming begins well before friends or family get as far as your foyer. There are a number of details to attend to in order to ensure that the path that leading to your door is warm, welcoming, and most importantly, safe. Study your home as you approach it from the street. Does the address show clearly? Are the numbers easy to find, well lit, and large enough to see from the street? This is not just a matter of convenience for guests but could also be a crucial and life-saving detail if the need arises to call emergency services such as the police, the fire department, or an ambulance to your home.

Can the path be easily differentiated from the front steps and driveway? This is especially important if the grade changes from one surface to another. If not, consider varying materials from drive to path to steps to visually delineate and define changes.

Is there sufficient light to find the way safely? Grade changes are the potential trouble spots and the logical location for outdoor light fixtures.

Can the doorbell or knocker be easily spotted? If the answer is no, consider upgrading the lighting at the front steps or installing a lighted doorbell button.

Is the bell or knocker audible, both inside and out, so that you and your guests can hear it? If it's hard to get to the door quickly, consider installing an intercom system that allows you to acknowledge guests quickly.

SMARTtip **Special Delivery**

If it's practical, install a mail slot that allows the mail to drop directly into a bin or basket in the foyer, or better yet, into the guest coat closet.

that pivots to reveal a shelf and several hangers makes a design statement as well as provides storage. The entry of a country-themed home might feature a rustic wooden bench that doubles as a table and seating.

Should a stairway run down to your entry foyer, and if the design of the surrounding spaces permit it, the triangular cavity of space beneath the stair can present an opportunity to increase your storage capacity significantly. A cabinetmaker or skilled carpenter can craft a combination of closets, drawers, or shelves to fit the area. These built-ins can service the entryway or any of the adjacent rooms, holding anything from clothes to books to bottles of wine.

FOYER FINESSE

Try to integrate the furnishings of the front entry with the tenor of your interior. This can be done without compromising the storage in the space. If you're a collector of antiques, an ornate coat rack with a built-in hinged-top bench fulfills several storage needs simultaneously. If the space just inside the front door is tiny, a shallow console table makes an attractive resting place for handbags and briefcases while coats are being shed. If it suits your climate, an umbrella stand is a thoughtful (not to mention pragmatic) touch that will save your floors from puddles while containing the unwieldy accessories. For the modernist with a bit more space, a stainless-steel-framed mirror

Above: The front entryway provides the first impression of your home, so choose furnishings and colors that complement the existing decor.

Right: In a busy household, the foyer might be the ideal out-of-the-way spot to locate a telephone for quiet conversation.

Sorting Mail

A mail-sorting-and-recycling system set up in the foyer or mudroom saves both time and steps and is an efficient way to eliminate clutter before it can gain a foothold in your house. With the current proliferation of promotional mailers, most households have pounds of unwanted paper delivered right to their doors each day. Set up a mail-sorting-and-recycling center near the door where the mail is picked up and there's no need to clutter up a desk, table, or kitchen counter with junk mail, even temporarily.

Should you go through the mail in the mudroom or the foyer? Which location to choose depends on where your mail is delivered. Many homeowners pick up their mail from a box located at the end of the driveway and come in a side or back door, making the mudroom the best spot. Others return home through the front entry to pick up mail left in a box there and would find a foyer mail-sorting station most useful.

Start with a few stackable bins in the mudroom or baskets stashed under a foyer console table. Even the drawers in an old desk or buffet can serve this function. Earmark one for recycling catalogs you don't want to keep, along with the colored-ink sections of the Sunday papers, too, if you are not a coupon clipper. Include another bin, basket, or drawer for catalogs you will look at when time permits. Color code or clearly label each so that you won't confuse them, or choose baskets with different colored or patterned liners. Next, toss junk mail and used envelopes in a wastebasket. You'll find many attractive models to suit all decors in a wide array of materials, including wood, rattan, wicker, and metal. Just be sure the container is large enough to handle the load from a few days. This collection can then be taken out the nearby door to a larger container for recycling or trash pickup.

In a more formal front entryway, look for attractive containers, fabric covered boxes, or fabric-lined baskets. Add a wall-hung hutch or cabinet with cubbies to leave mail for each family member. After you've trimmed down the pile, bring only the necessary pieces into the main part of the house.

Above: Bins, boxes, and baskets can serve many functions, including corralling paper in the foyer.

Left: Provide a rack or cubbies to hold incoming mail.

Above: Don't have an entry? Create the sense of one on the wall nearest the door. Here the homeowner used a simple bench to hold baskets and added hanging pegs and a message board.

Above right: Make entryway storage easy for kids to use. Include sturdy drawers, open bins, hooks they can reach, and a spot dedicated to odd-shaped or bulky sports gear to help keep the area neat.

SMARTtip Mail Drop

Create a mail drop-off point at the entry you use most often. If it's the front door, an elegant silver bowl or artisan-made basket could serve this purpose; in the mudroom, a wooden wall caddy can be painted or stained in a coordinating color.

MUDROOMS WITHOUT MADNESS

At the other end of the house, the mudroom is made to accommodate a rugged, regular stampede of kids, dogs, and deliveries. In these spaces, durability may trump high design. If a bank of conventional closets is installed in a busy mudroom, it's not hard to imagine the chaotic scenario that could erupt on a Saturday morning: little fingers getting pinched in the doors, junior's favorite cap falling into the dark depths of the back of the closet, and you straining to reach your jacket and scarf, which have migrated to the far end.

You can avoid this by using an open outerwear storage system, which features a series of simple pegs and hooks that can be installed right on the wall. While hangers should be used to help preserve the shape of dress coats and wraps, more casual wear like sweaters, parkas, and jean jackets can withstand hanging from the neck loop with no ill effects. Hats and scarves can be stashed on open shelves or hooks where they can air out. Held together with clothespins, mittens and gloves can remain paired while they dry.

When you're designing your mudroom or back entry, there are a few other helpful things to keep in mind.

Mudroom Locations. Make sure it's easy to negotiate. Just inside the back or side door, off the family room or

Seating and Set-Down Areas. Provide a roomy bench at a height that's comfortable for all to use when changing from their shoes into boots. Box it in so that the base becomes a storage chest, or leave it open so that you can slide a low waterproof basket or tray underneath. A built-in bench that's long enough for two or three people to sit down simultaneously is ideal. But don't despair if you're short on space—even in a minimal, make-do mudroom, the addition of a stool will improve both its comfort and its functionality.

Open Cubbies. Open cubbies make it easy to spot things fast. If they conflict with your style, choose closed lockers, perhaps color-coded for each child to stash coats, hats, mittens, a backpack or book bag, shoes, and rain gear. Include child-high pegs or hooks and a hanging pole for adult's coats. Be sure you plan for possible family expansion and for the inevitable growth of little ones, and provide space to raise the hooks as needed.

kitchen is ideal. Use sturdy, easy-to-clean flooring, such as natural stone or ceramic tile. Avoid highly glazed tiles or stone, which are slippery when wet. Before you buy any flooring for use in a mudroom (or foyer), take a sample home and mist it with water to test it. Also, ask the salesperson for its slip-resistance rating.

Pet Accommodations. Incorporate a niche into the mudroom for you pet's food and water. Provide a hook for the dog's leash and a bin for pet toys. Add an open bench and consider it the ideal place to tuck the cat or dog bed when not in use.

Opposite: The mudroom is a convenient spot to provide food and water for pets when they come in from outdoors.

Above: Store less frequently used items and out-of-season clothing on the upper shelves. Everything that gets daily use should be convenient and reachable.

Right: This back entry hall is informal but pretty. An oversized bench with hooks organizes everything.

SMARTtip Clean Sweep

If you're short on utility closet space, hang a broom and dustpan or a small cordless vacuum in the mudroom. It's a logical location for these items because you'll use them there frequently.

For the avalanche of odd-shaped articles—backpacks and book bags, baseball bats, galoshes, and the occasional soccer ball—that invade the mudroom but aren't suitable for hanging, sturdy bins are the first line of defense. As always, measure the items that you know or anticipate will be making an appearance in the mudroom and then find appropriately sized containers for them. There's no feeling more deflating than realizing that your carefully selected rattan market basket can accommodate only one rollerblade rather than a pair.

Organize the containers on shelves that span a variety of heights: some that are just inches off the floor up to about waist-level are best for things that are used frequently, while overhead spaces should be reserved for stuff that only sees sporadic activity.

Install a bulletin board or a chalkboard. Use it for posting schedules for sports, household chore charts, and other information that family members refer to frequently. Hanging it by the mudroom door prevents dirty, cleated feet from trekking further into the house to check on the time for next week's game. There's no reason why you can't enhance its usefulness beyond being just a sign post, though; screw a couple of hooks to the frame to hold spare keys to the garden shed, bike lock, or garage, and add a narrow ledge to the top or bottom of the board to display a photo or keepsake.

In geographic areas that receive lots of snow or rain, include a towel warmer. Kids can use it to hang up wet snowsuits and mittens for fast, gentle drying. And look for a spot to stash a laundry basket in the mudroom for really dirty items like wet socks, gardening clothes, or pool towels.

Finally, if at all possible, locate a powder room near the mudroom. That way, children, guests at outdoor parties, or the gardener in the family can make a quick trip inside and not track mud through the house.

Above: Closed cabinets make a neat appearance in a more formal space.

Left: Open cubbies and accessible hooks mean kids are more likely to hang up their gear. Baskets are perfect containers for mittens, scarves, and hats.

Opposite Right: A bench makes it easier for everyone in the family to put on their boots.

To get started on reorganizing your entry hall or mudroom, follow these Smart Steps.

ONE **Eliminate.** Because they're entry points, it's natural that a lot of extraneous items accumulate in the foyer and mudroom. At one time or another, just about everyone is guilty of letting a week's worth of junk mail pile up on the table by the front door; stashing the dry cleaning in the coat closet until you have a chance to run it upstairs, of course; or putting the kid-next-door's skateboard in the mudroom where it will likely sit for a month until he remembers to pick it up. Storage slip-ups like these cripple effective organization. Return everything that doesn't have a rightful claim to entryway space to its logical home.

TWO **Assess.** With the inappropriate things edited, take stock of what remains in the coat closet or mudroom. Check for clothes that need mending or cleaning. Toss out broken umbrellas, missing mittens, and any other items that have outlived their use. Donate gently worn jackets and coats to a charitable organization.

THREE **Upgrade your organizing scheme.** For instance, forsake wire hangers and ensure there's an adequate number of sturdy wooden ones for coats. Rather than a central catchall for caps, scarves, and gloves, assign a basket to each member of the household. Invest in a shoe rack to keep garden clogs and sneakers neatly paired.

CHAPTER 3

IDEAS FOR THE KITCHEN

- FLOOR-PLAN BASICS
- CABINET OPTIONS
- COUNTERTOP STORAGE
- WALL STORAGE

In 1976, that time-honored tome *The Joy of Cooking* tallied 291 items that comprised the basic *batterie du cuisine* in the average kitchen. Some two decades later, the National Kitchen & Bath Association (NKBA), a professional trade organization, surveyed the average North American kitchen and found 791 pots, pans, tools, glasses, and dishes. And in the larder they counted 18 cans, 23 spices, and 6 boxes of cereal. Even though that timeline spans a mere 20 years, the conclusion is clear: there's a lot of stuff to store in the kitchen. And if the kitchen was not originally designed to handle it all, those items offer the potential to spill onto the countertop and devour workspace. Despite the advent of multipurpose appliances, such as the food processor, electric skillet, and toaster oven, the growth trend in kitchen gadgetry continues upward. While the doughnut cutter may no longer be the cooking essential that it was in the 1950s, an avalanche of new gizmos are vying for a place in your cabinets and drawers. If you must possess an automatic pineapple corer, realize there is a finite amount of space in the kitchen. Be discerning and follow one of the basic rules for keeping clutter at bay: get rid of one old item for every new one you acquire. Stop hoarding what you don't use; if you own a microwave—and most people do—toss the popcorn popper. This chapter will show you lots of ways to make more room in the kitchen.

FLOOR-PLAN BASICS

Architects and professional kitchen designers often field the same question from their clients, "What kitchen floor plan offers the most potential for storage?" The answer: None of them.

Every home has a unique set of variables that dictates to a large extent exactly how much capacity a kitchen can possess. For instance, a room that is too confining to accommodate the minimum recommended work-aisle width of 36 inches wouldn't be able to support a storage-rich center island. Any windows in the kitchen will limit the use of full-size wall cabinets, just as doorways interrupt runs of both base and wall cabinetry. And the location of necessary basic utilities—electrical wiring, and plumbing supply and waste lines—often predetermines the location of sinks, dishwashers, and major cooking appliances.

SPOT ON STORAGE

Point-of-use storage, which saves steps and time, is of utmost importance in the kitchen and is the common denominator in all well-planned designs, no matter how the space has been configured. Regardless of whether you have a corridor-like galley layout, or an L-, U-, or G-shape plan, it's always smart to keep everyday cookware near the range, dishes and glasses close to the sink and dishwasher, and foodstuffs in between these workstations.

While there is no one perfect layout, there is a simple appraisal process that's invaluable for defining your personal kitchen storage needs.

ONE Analyze your shopping patterns. Do you buy staples in bulk every other week, make daily trips to the greengrocer for the freshest produce, or go to the supermarket on an as-needed basis? How you shop and what items you keep on hand determine the best place to locate and how to structure your pantry.

TWO Know your cooking habits. Are weekday dinners microwave affairs or three courses from scratch? Do you bake throughout the year or only around holidays and birthdays? Are veggie stir-fry meals a family favorite, or do you cook for a meat-and-potatoes crowd? Is the pressure cooker or the slow cooker used on a regular basis? You'll gain insight into how to effectively store your pans, pots, and equipment with a grasp of how and what you cook.

SMARTtip Space Saver

On the shelf or in the fridge, square and rectangular storage containers are more space-efficient than round ones.

Opposite bottom: A custom plate rack on the wall above the sink in this kitchen saves steps.

Left: A grid of cubbies gives this countertop "wine cellar" a graphic presence.

Below: To keep kids out of the work aisle, incorporate undercounter storage for snacks at the end of an island.

THREE Take stock of the contents of your cupboards. Are you big on canned foods, or are frozen foods a mainstay of the menu? Do you like to toss a pinch or two of exotic seasonings into foods as they cook, or is a bottle of Tabasco about as wild as tastes go in your home? Do leftovers play a recurring role? Do you favor the large economy size for your family of five or six? Must you store food for two finicky cats and a 90-pound dog along with the human members of your family? Make note of what items you like to keep on hand.

FOUR Scrutinize your cleanup methods. Do dishes air-dry on a sink-side rack after being hand washed? Do you fill up the dishwasher over the course of the day and run it overnight, every night? Do you use it more or less frequently than that? Your answers to these questions will indicate dish- and glassware storage needs.

Left: A toekick drawer can be used in many ways. This one has been fitted with a collapsible stepladder.

Below: An open cabinet in the cleanup island provides a discreet place for dish towels.

CABINET OPTIONS

To make a systematic survey of the storage needs and opportunities in your kitchen, start with the cabinets, beginning at the bottom and working your way up.

A European innovation that is now finding a more appreciative audience on this side of the pond is the storage plinth. Also known as the toekick, this 5-inch-tall slot of space beneath the base cabinets can be put to work by incorporating shallow drawers. These drawers can hold flat articles that are fairly large—examples include cookie sheets and wire cooling racks, serving platters, a collapsible stepstool, folded kitchen towels, and newspapers or magazines bound for recycling.

BASE CABINETS

Moving up to examine the foundation of kitchen storage, base cabinets have undergone some progressive changes in the past few years. Comprising cupboards, drawers, and hybrid pullout units, these are the best and most likely places for storing heavy and bulky items. Small appliances that aren't used daily—such as blenders and food processors—pots, pans, and bakeware are the most popular occupants of these cabinets.

There are two types of cabinet configurations: straight runs and corner units. Standard straight-run base units (called stock cabinets in the trade) measure 24 inches deep, and their widths are set in 3-inch increments that range from 9 to 45 inches. Fixed shelves—which have subjected cooks to spine-twisting contortions for too many years—are becoming a thing of the past, with more ergonomically sensitive and sensible rollout shelves or trays taking their place. These optional enhancements are inexpensive and easy to retrofit into existing cabinets. Adding them will immediately improve the storage performance of any kitchen without undergoing a major renovation.

Dish Up Storage

For everyday dishes, here are several appealing approaches to storage:

- Store them in large, deep drawers. Line the bottom of the drawers with pegboard, and use movable pegs to corral plates and bowls in neat stacks.
- Plate racks, on their own or integrated into a bank of cabinetry, put your dishware on display while keeping it handy.
- If you intend to use a built-in plate rack for drying your dishes, make sure it's installed where the wet dishes can drip into the sink, either directly or by means of a drainboard.
- Should you choose to keep dishes in a cupboard, check out the array of minishelves that allow you to separately stack plates of different diameters so that you can easily get access to them one at a time.
- A word about glass-fronted cabinets: unless you have immaculately kept cupboards, artfully filled with beautiful glassware and dishes, think twice before giving the all-clear on this door-style option. Instead, consider using seeded, ribbed, frosted, or tinted glass panels on the doors. You'll still reap the benefits from a lighter look, but you won't have to suffer the full exposure of your cabinets' not too neat or attractive contents.

Above: These sturdy cabinet drawers can store heavy dishes. Removable dividers let you configure interiors.

DRAWERS

Within a straight expanse of cabinetry, deep drawers are increasingly offered as an appealing alternative to cupboards for several reasons. First, they conserve motion: only one action is required to get access to drawers, versus two—opening the door and bending to see inside—for cabinets with doors. Full-extension glides that allow the drawers to be pulled all the way out, thus bringing the contents to you, make it easier to see and reach what's inside. Finally, deep drawers can generally support more weight than slide-out shelves. If and when you plan to remodel your kitchen, consider including at least some large deep drawers.

Opposite: Wicker drawers are both practical and pretty.

Below: A tilt-out panel located in front of the sink is a perfect example of how to make good use of every inch of space.

Drawers can also be fitted with quite an assortment of accessories that can be tailored to your gastronomic interests. Bakers will find covered breadbox inserts in clay or metal handy for keeping the fruits of their labors fresh. Acrylic or stainless-steel bins for flour and grains keep canisters off the counter and a ready supply on hand.

BASKETS

Some cabinet manufacturers offer woven baskets dropped into a wooden frame that fits into side-mounted drawer slides. In a kitchen with a rustic or traditional theme, a stack of two or three of these can provide convenient pull-out ventilated storage for certain varieties of produce while adding an interesting note of texture to the room.

Another intersection of storage and style are drawers with glass false fronts. These can be filled with colorful dried beans, pasta in curious shapes, doggie treats, jelly beans—anything that enhances the character of your kitchen and complements the design of the room.

Trash Talking

Because trash and recycling bins are used several times each day during preparations for meals and snacks, the location of each is an important consideration. Aim to make recycling convenient, and it becomes less of a chore and your family will find it easier to participate. Some tips:

- Plan a cutout in the countertop that allows you to drop vegetable peels and other nonprotein food scraps into an undercounter bin that can be carried to the compost pile daily.
- Concealed trash bins that tilt out or pull out on a platform installed on drawer slides not only save floor space and keep pets out of the trash but conserve time and motion. You'll find many configurations, including models that hide behind a single cabinet door and conceal from one to three bins, so you can recycle at the same spot where you dispose of trash.
- If local recycling requirements call for less mingling and more sorting of recycled items, opt for four bins. But you'll need to stash these behind two cabinet doors, not one.
- Choose bins in sizes that suit how much recyclable trash you actually generate. A container that's too small will mean more trips to the outdoor recycling bins.
- Conserve space in the recycling bin by flattening plastic bottles and cardboard packages.
- Keep the box of trash bags at the bottom of the can. You'll always have one handy when changing bags, and you will free up a little bit of drawer space.
- Try to locate the trash anywhere but in the cabinet under the sink so that whoever does the dishes has an unobstructed place to stand.

Right: Glide-out trash receptacles utilize the full depth of the base cabinets.

Below: Recycling is quick, convenient, and concealed using multiple collection bins.

SMART tip Scraps

If your kitchen has a pullout chopping board, consider installing a pullout trash bin in the cupboard below it. Clearing cuttings off the board becomes a one-step operation. Chose two bins, and earmark one for trash and one for scraps destined for the compost pile.

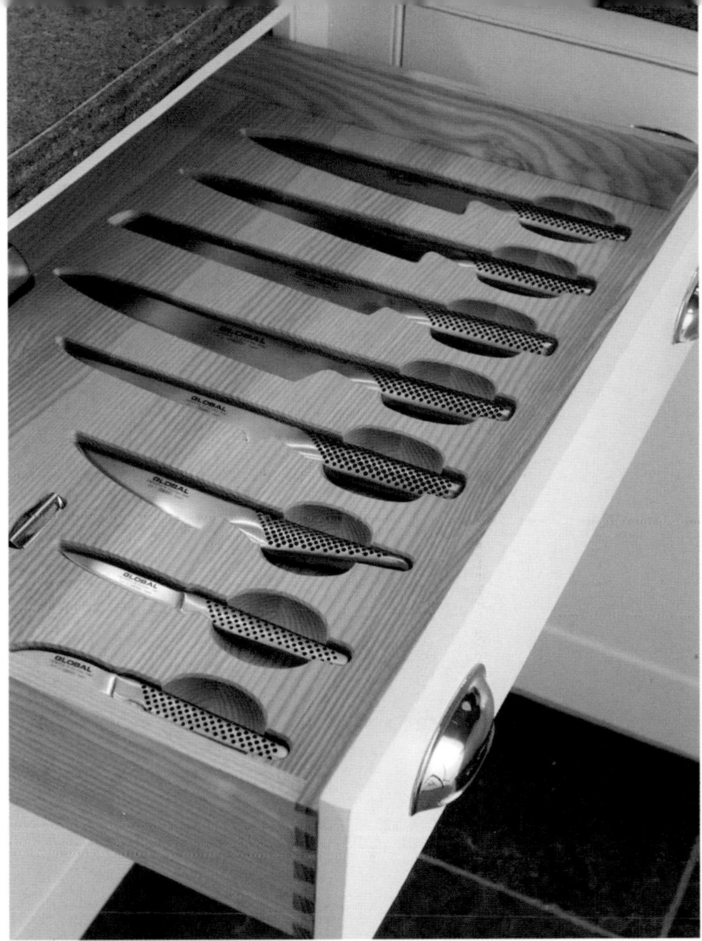

INSERTS

Standard 5-inch-deep drawers remain a vital staple in the kitchen. Scaled for utensils and silverware, even existing drawer storage can be maximized with segmented or tiered cutlery inserts. Look for trays with adjustable compartments; molded all-in-one designs are sometimes too limiting. Another variation on this option is to use individual bins that hook together; you configure them to fit your needs. At the high end of the market, drawers can be fitted with wooden inserts that have precisely scribed recesses for each tool stored—pricey but beautiful examples of the wood-worker's craft and a storage reward for the discerning chef.

Above left: Organized by design: custom cutlery cutouts protect knives—and hands—from nicks.

Left: Everyday silverware can be kept tidy in a segmented drawer

Top: Behind closed doors, a coffee machine and all of its accoutrements are ready to go. Slots overhead hold trays and shallow pans.

Above: Space next to the wall ovens is used as a "broom closet."

Above top right: Tiers of bottle racks stretch this cabinet's storage.

Above middle right: Long tools and implements hang out here.

Right: Towels stay clean and dry in this pullout.

Opposite: Herbs and spices are stowed stove side, where they're frequently used during cooking.

PULLOUT CABINETS

Pullout cabinets combine the convenience of drawers with the capacity of cupboards. They can range from a pair of narrow base-cabinet spice units that conveniently flank the stove to a towering 6-foot-tall pantry that can house just about everything.

Such full-height cabinets should be organized following basic storage principles: store the larger, heavier articles at the bottom, and put frequently used items on the shelves that correspond to the space from your knees to your shoulder height. And if possible, opt for adjustable shelving so you have maximum storage flexibility.

Store food staples in groups. Some examples include locating baking ingredients on one shelf, and cereals and breakfast items on another. Set aside one shelf for snacks, another for oils and vinegars, and yet another for dry items such as rice, grains, and pasta. If you always keep the same items in the same location, everyone in the family can find them quickly and return them to the right spot later. Store less frequently used items and back-up supplies toward the rear of the cabinet shelf.

SMARTtip Convenience

Putting a drawer right beneath a built-in microwave lets you keep small plastic containers and lids conveniently at hand.

SMARTtip Deep Thoughts

Match the size of the item to the size of the cabinet or drawer. Don't fill a deep drawer with piles of small utensils and gadgets. Save it for the bulky salad spinner and large serving bowls or appliances.

CORNERS

The 90-degree turn-of-a-corner cabinet is by nature space squandering, leaving the curved wedge of room at the rear of the corner empty as well as almost completely out of reach. A 45-degree corner base cabinet is more forgiving in its frontal orientation, but its primary benefit is really felt at the countertop level, where the additional surface area it provides can accommodate a cooktop or sink.

The door treatments for corner cabinets differ on a case-by-case basis and may affect how efficiently you can make use of the cabinet. A pair of doors may split open down the center. In kitchens with clearance issues, a double-hinged door can open, fold in on itself, and then swing aside. In some instances, there may be only one door to a corner cabinet, a particularly uncomfortable condition that's known as a "blind corner."

Left: A full-height pantry cabinet reclaims an otherwise underutilized corner of the kitchen.

Left: Even awkward angles can supply a slice of productive storage.

Below: In a 45-degree corner, drawers are easily accessible.

While this may sound ominous for storage possibilities, the situation is salvageable. Inserts—those wire, plastic, or wood shelves, spinners, and sliders that can convert an empty-box cabinet into a shining example of custom-made storage—will rescue the most recalcitrant corner. Whether ordered as part of a new kitchen or slipped into existing cabinets, they can bring dead space to life or extend the efficiency of storage that's not up to snuff.

There are numerous forms of corner-centric inserts. One solution to a blind corner is to fit it with what's sometimes called a "magic corner" by those in the kitchen-design trade. This is a set of shelves that's jointed in the middle; with one end attached to the corner-cabinet door, the shelves automatically unfold outside the cabinet when the door is opened. Other examples of angular space saviors include two- or three-level carousels and lazy Susans. The former, which is also fastened to the inside of the cabinet door, rotates 270 degrees; the latter spins a full 360 degrees. A modification of the Susan is a model that comes with lidded storage containers shaped like slices of pie.

Finally, a spinning, three-bin recycling center may be the best use of a corner base cabinet. Accessibility isn't an issue, as each container rotates to the fore of the cupboard.

COUNTERTOP STORAGE

"Counter surfaces are not to be used as storage areas," say some experts. Is that an inviolable manifesto or an organizational myth? A little of both, actually.

Kitchen counters are typically 24 inches deep, and the leading 18 inches is the active territory of most prep tasks. That part of the surface is literally within a comfortable arm's reach and can easily be lit with under-cabinet lighting. Keep this space clear, and use the 6 inches of counter nearest the wall for items that you use daily, such as the coffeemaker or the toaster.

APPLIANCE GARAGES

An appliance garage can prevent countertop storage space from looking too jumbled. When this cabinetry concept was first introduced, it wasn't a particularly pretty sight: a clunky box pushed into the corner of the counter that usually featured a wooden tambour door, which had a tendency to stick. (Invariably, the coffeemaker resided there.)

But with advances in cabinet hardware come advances in design. Hinged panel doors that flip up to open, or doors that slide back along the sides of the cabinet, have opened up more attractive appliance-garage possibilities. If building codes in your area allow, you may be able to put an electrical outlet inside the garage.

Here's a novel, more architectural twist on countertop storage. Lately, there's been a lot of interest in setting a couple of shallow drawers right on the counter, topping them with an elongated hanging wall cabinet. This column-like design not only adds a vertical note to the kitchen, but the assembly is a deft combination of storage types that's responsive to the needs of the user.

Left: No heavy lifting here. This stand mixer can just slide out of its appliance garage for use. The hinged door flips up for easy access into the cabinet.

Left: The cook's favorites are kept in a tiled niche behind the cooktop.

WALL STORAGE

A simple way to get more storage mileage out of a standard 4-inch-tall backsplash is to top it with a 3-inch-wide ledge. This makes a fine perch for small collectibles or jars of herbs and seasonings, and lends a custom finish to an otherwise boring detail.

RAILS AND RODS

Rail or rod systems are not at all difficult to install (even on tiled surfaces). Some have sets of matching specialized accessories from coffee filter holders to knife racks to wine bottles and shelves; others supply more generic storage with the help of S-hooks and hanging bins.

Give some thought to where's really the best place to locate them. While having ladles, tongs, and mixing spoons suspended close to the cooktop sounds like a great idea—and all those gleaming utensils look so professional—there's a potential drawback. They'll be directly exposed to steam and grease. If you don't mind the additional cleanup, you'll appreciate the convenience; if you do, look elsewhere in your kitchen to apply this kind of storage.

WALL CABINETS

Unlike base cabinets, where what you see is what you get, wall cabinets can take one of several paths in terms of basic installation options.

The soffits—the area between just below the ceiling and above the wall cabinets—can be boxed in to be flush with the face of the cabinets or remain open. The first treatment gives a clean, built-in look to the cabinetry but eliminates what amounts to a commodious, yet inaccessible, shelf. An open soffit, on the other hand, leaves the tops of the wall cabinets unenclosed, and so depending on which way you tend to look at collectibles on display, provides either a spacious band of high-level display space or a roosting spot for dirt and grime.

OPEN SHELVES

A third alternative for wall storage is open shelves. While they are perfect for putting your collection of majolica platters or antique coffee grinders on exhibit, they are susceptible to collecting dust. Used as an accent element, they give visual relief to the monolithic look of solid-front cabinets.

Even though they're just 12 inches deep, wall cupboards have an uncanny way of swallowing up just the item you're trying to find. Luckily, just as with base cabinets, there's now an abundance of storage-supplementing inserts available for wall-hung designs.

Bottle and Jar Organizers. Bottles and jars revolve into view when placed on a mini lazy Susan. Stair-step organizers literally boost the visibility of back-of-the-cabinet contents. For those who need a bit of extra help in reaching upper shelves, there's a double-decker insert that pulls down and out of the cabinet to make life easier.

Storage for Spices. The inside of the upper cabinet doors is a great spot for storing spices. Look in retail storage supply stores and catalogs for a variety of bins and baskets designed to attach to the inside of the doors. Before installing one of those handy inside-of-the-door shelf units or baskets, make sure it's positioned clear of the shelves inside the cabinet. If it's not, the door won't close properly.

Whatever your preferred storage method for herbs, spices, and seasonings—in a drawer, on the wall, in a countertop rack—organize them alphabetically so you can quickly find what you're looking for. They maintain flavor and freshness best if they're kept away from heat and light.

Ceiling-Hung Storage. Occupying a middle ground between wall cupboards and overhead storage are peninsula cabinets, so named for the floor-plan feature above which they customarily hang. These ceiling-mounted units are most at home in open or semi-open spaces, so they might not be the first resort for interior kitchens.

Best suspended over an island or peninsula to avoid banging your head, hanging pot racks offer practical storage as well as an eye-pleasing focal point to the kitchen. If you've got lots of pots, shop around for a model that has a center shelf as well as hooks, or divvy up your collection by size or material, placing them on more than one rack. Take special care to ensure any hanging rack is secured to structural members in the ceiling, and resist the urge to position it too close to the burners, as your pans will be enveloped by greasy cooking vapors.

Right: With open shelves, cabinets, drawers, a retractable towel rod, and a plate rack, this kitchen is a storage sampler.

CHAPTER 4

LIVING AND FAMILY ROOMS

- FURNITURE SMARTS
- BUILT-INS
- ART AND COLLECTIONS

People come together in the living and family rooms to mix and mingle. That's why organization is so important to the rooms' design success. Of the two, living rooms are typically more formal and mainly reserved for company in some households. Whichever way you decorate the living room in your home, aim for an inviting space that mirrors your personality, interests, and style. Keep clutter at bay so that people can actually see those qualities. Create comfort with appropriately scaled furniture, and please the eye by thoughtfully showcasing art and accessories. The same applies to the casual living space provided by family rooms—perhaps even more so because this is where it all happens, every day.

So how does making smart choices in storage affect your decorating plans? First, space is a factor to be considered when choosing furniture and its placement. Then there is the style issue: will you rely on open or closed storage, or a mixture of the two? Lovers of formal interiors may not gain style points if the TV sits starkly out in the open, for example, and the less-is-more modernist would likely prefer to keep something like a set of leather-bound classic books hidden behind cabinet doors. The suggestions and photos on the following pages will help you define the type of organization needed for these rooms and inspire you with ideas for achieving it.

FURNITURE SMARTS

Whether it's the living room, the den, or the family room, this public room is always on display. Keep it comfortable and tidy by avoiding clutter. Make an effort to put things away. Don't leave magazines or videos lying about on tabletops or the floor. Adopt the "less is more" philosophy. After you read a magazine, throw it away or find a place to store back issues of periodicals. Rent, don't buy, videos unless you have a cabinet for storing them. Edit your existing furniture. If the room is crowded, keep only those pieces that suit the scale of the room. Folding pieces that you can store in the attic or the garage can come to the rescue as needed when you entertain.

Below: Shelves on either side of a fireplace can show off collectibles and house books, CDs, or videos. Stacked end tables conserve space.

SMARTtip Art of Boxing

Keep a small scissors in a pretty box that you can keep on display in the living or family room. Use it to clip coupons or recipes from newspapers and magazines.

CHOOSING AND USING INDIVIDUAL PIECES WISELY

One way to declutter living spaces is to to use furniture pieces that can serve more than one function. Make an unofficial declaration that no table of any type will be allowed into the living room unless it has at least one shelf or drawer. Change traditional end tables to small chests or cabinets that incorporate a bit of extra concealed storage.

Consider freeing up the surface of the end tables by getting rid of lamps and replacing them with wall-mounted swing-arm fixtures. (A bonus: these models are more convenient for reading, as you can focus the light directly on the page.) The coffee table should be commodious; in an ideal world, it would be sufficiently spacious so you would be able to retire your end tables altogether. Look for one with doors or drawers. Cushy ottomans with storage cavities inside can hold neatly folded throws and out-of-season slipcovers with no one the wiser.

Make or buy low shelving units that will fit under your windows as a spot for stashing toys, board games, or books and locating a lamp.

Above: Hide the TV and its related gear in a closed cabinet if you want to prevent the big black box from dominating the room.

Below: Round out storage by mixing in pieces, such as boxes or trunks, that can double as tables. Use trays to contain tabletop items.

Making Music

One of the most common items to store in a den, living, or family room is a CD collection. But nothing deters use of the collection more than a messy jumble of discs. Here are a few tips for storing them that will protect them and keep them organized.

- Keep CDs accessible, though not necessarily on view. Before you buy a CD storage rack or organizer, eliminate what you don't want to keep. Count what's left; then buy something that will accommodate what you own and allow for new purchases in the future. Do this periodically.
- Avoid stacking CDs one on top of the other so that you don't have to move 10 of them to get to the one you want. Instead, always store CDs in their cases, spine out, so you can read the titles. A little-used corner might be the perfect place for a tall storage cabinet. Or use a small chest with several drawers that are the right size for CDs. If there is a closet in the room, purchase an over-the-door CD rack.
- Yes, it may sound obsessive, but if you organize CDs by category, it will be easier to find the jazz, rock, classical, or country when you're in the mood. Alphabetize by artist within category.
- Provide adequate lighting in or near the storage area so you can read the spines. This can be as simple as installing a larger-wattage bulb in a nearby lamp or buying a lamp with a three-way switch, so you can brighten the light when needed.

LOOK UP

Vertical storage is the workhorse of any room. If your living or family room is a collection of sofas and chairs, with little space available for storage pieces, consider putting the wall space to work by adding shelves. "Wall units" have come a long way from when the term meant heavy, dully designed monoliths in one or two equally uninspired finishes: dark brown or light brown. Today, furniture designs have lightened up considerably, giving you quite the number of choices in decor at every price point.

Storage can be found in the form of grids, ladderlike or lean-to shelves, and hanging or cantilevered units, to name just a few of the new configurations that allow you to think well outside the box. The range of materials has also expanded, with glass, metal, hi-tech polymers, and even cardboard joining wood. The array of finishes and species has expanded as well. Don't rule out custom shelves, either.

CREATING INTEREST

In the pursuit of order, it's important to remember variety. A mix of open shelving and closed cabinetry will give the room a more sophisticated appearance, while serving different types of storage needs. Fragile collectible items can be protected from dust and damage yet still be easy to see when they're kept safely under or behind glass. Solid doors can hide books with less-than-perfect bindings, mismatched audio components, or anything that should be handy but not left on view. Otherwise put these items into attractive baskets that fit into the cabinet. That way you can camouflage the unsightlies with a good-looking wicker display. For small items, use ceramic pots, bowls, or jars with a matching motif or color.

Vary the heights of the wall storage for the most pleasing look. One or two floor-to-ceiling components are fine, but if you use too many of them, your room could quickly look crowded again, especially if it's small. Remember, this isn't a closet. Be realistic about how much stuff to keep in the room. As an alternative use a low bookcase (two or three shelves) for open displays.

Opposite: Tall dark-wood cabinets are perfectly in proportion to the massive fireplace that they flank in this room where the ceiling height is dramatic.

BUILT-INS

By using a little imagination with cabinetry, you can enhance the architectural appeal of your living room while creating storage with built-in units. If the room has an existing focal point—a fireplace or a dramatic window, for example—cabinetry and shelving can be configured around it. A hearth-side inglenook or a cozy window seat can be constructed from scratch or by inventively using standard kitchen cabinetry modules. Built-in storage is most effective and pleasing in this application, because it becomes a permanent feature in the room rather than an afterthought. Use moldings and hardware to tie in the design of the built-ins to other features in the room.

Another location to consider enhancing with built-ins is around the entrance to the room. Shallow shelves built into the wall on either side and above the doorway look dramatic while providing handy niches for collections, books, CDs, DVDs, compact speakers, or anything else you can fit into them. Use small low-voltage light fixtures to add extra style.

Opposite: Use moldings, arches, and trim to add a finishing touch to built-in storage or display shelves.

Right: Custom-built shelving creates a niche for the sofa in this living room.

Below left: Compact low-voltage lighting heightens the design drama of open shelves that were built to house audio components and a music collection in this room.

Below right: Cabinets were built into the wall below the loft landing of this soaring open-plan family room.

SMARTtip Adaptive Reuse

If your living room features a faux fireplace or a fireplace that's not used, put it to work as a bend-the-rules storage niche. Outfit the opening with a wine rack, for example. Be sure to measure the opening before you do any shopping.

One thing that is unlikely to change is the proliferation of remote controls. Keep them organized by training all the channel surfers in your home to stash them in the same basket. Better yet, invest in a single universal control, and say adios to the lot of them.

MAKING ROOM FOR THE TV

It's been common practice to conceal the TV and its ever-growing related apparatus—VCR, cable box, video game unit, DVD or DVR, and additional speakers—in built-in cabinets or an armoire that coordinates with the room's interior design. Closed cabinets are fitted with wraparound hinges that permit the doors to open flat against the walls of the unit for unobscured viewing; adjustable shelves and cutouts in the back panel allow for cord entry and ventilation—electronics produce a lot of heat while you're running them.

A change in viewing habits may be in the air, especially because slimmed-down flat-screen plasma TVs and LCD screens are becoming affordable and popular. These thin TVs can be installed right on the wall, on a shelf, or inside a shallow cabinet.

Above and above left: In this sleek space the large screen TV actually becomes part of an architectural element when it disappears behind retractable doors.

Left: In keeping with this home's Southwest architecture, pine was used to make shelves that fit nicely into an otherwise useless wall between the fireplace and doors.

Below: Toss books that are waiting to be read or returned to the library in a large basket that you can slide under an end table.

SMARTtip In and Out

There is a way to stem the never-ending buildup of back issues of all the magazines that come in the mail. Make a hard-and-fast rule for everyone in your household: throw out the last issue as soon as the new one arrives in the mail.

MANAGING MAGAZINES

Sorry, stuffing magazines under the sofa seat cushion does not qualify as smart storage. To keep the Sunday papers and mail-order catalogs from encroaching further upon the living room, there are a couple measures you can take.

Store magazines upright. That will minimize the amount of flat space they consume; a conventional standing rack or a vertical wall file will hold the most reading material in the least amount of space. Naturally, the alternative is to deposit publications in an attractive box or basket and to slip it under a table or onto a deep shelf. However, none of these methods will be effective unless you diligently ferry back issues into the recycling bin.

SMARTtip Square Off

When hanging pictures on a wall, line them up along their top edges rather than the bottom of the frames. It creates a more polished presentation.

ART AND COLLECTIONS

Of all the areas in a home, the living room is the most appropriate place to put quality artwork on display. Before you do, a little curatorial housekeeping is almost always in order, however.

Paintings are what usually come to mind first when considering art for display at home. These can be original works or high-quality reproduction prints, but not the kids' school art, which is better suited to the kitchen or perhaps a scrapbook that's kept in the family room. Sculpture is another category that lends itself to display. Even functional items of quality (textiles, such as quilts, rugs, or tapestries, or antique architectural ornaments, for example) can be art worthy if they are displayed tastefully. But remember: nothing dilutes the impact of a collection more than an inferior piece; anything called a "tchotchke" is not art pottery.

SMARTtip Separate Spaces

If you're lucky enough to have a large living room, adopt a trick from urban loft-dwellers: use a freestanding shelving unit or étagère that's open on both sides as a room divider. It gently segments the space without sacrificing storage.

Below: Numerous pieces in a thoughtful arrangement never look cluttered.

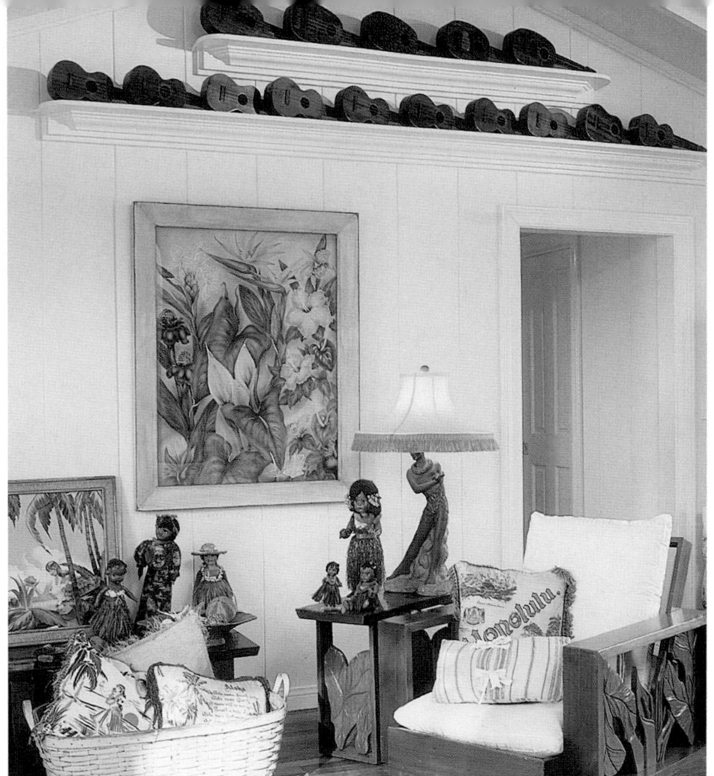

Above: Show off a collection to its best advantage by massing all the items in one location. Note how white walls make the colors pop into view.

Below: Collections are always evolving, so display facilities should be adjustable. These shelves are able to accommodate wooden ducks of various sizes.

Above: An odd-shaped space under a sloped ceiling is put to excellent use as a place to show off a collection of vintage ukuleles.

Below: Uniformity in both the shelf heights and the objects on display creates a pleasing composition that becomes a source of visual interest and conversation in this room.

ARRANGING WALL ART

Framed photos or paintings can be arranged on the wall singly or in choreographed clusters. But before you start rapping the walls for studs and tapping nails into them, a little planning is in order.

Trace templates on kraft paper for each piece you want to hang; then affix them with drafting tape to the wall in different designs. Once you find an arrangement that works for you, go ahead and reach for the hammer.

In a less traditional approach, lean framed pieces against the wall as they rest on decorative ledges or a mantel. This tactic works especially well if you are strapped for open expanses of wall area but have a large number of photos or paintings that you want to put on display. You can change the exhibition anytime you want by pulling out the nails; spackling, sanding, and painting over holes; and laying out a new artful scheme.

There is no one "right way" to hang a collection of art. Try arranging paper templates of the pieces until you find a layout that pleases you.

Light a Collection

Casting your collections in the best light is an intrinsic part of an effective display. Contemplate how you want your displays to be perceived: do you want to accent one special piece or several? A spotlight, positioned at a 30-degree angle to your display, is your answer. If you prefer a more ambient wash of light to show off your collection, or you'd rather emphasize texture, transparency, or some other nuance in the artwork, pay a visit to a reputable showroom and meet with an accredited lighting designer.

- **Track Lighting.** The versatility of track lighting makes it appealing to people who change their wall displays on a regular basis. They are surface mounted, so installing them is typically less involved than hard-wiring a new circuit. Track systems come in both standard and low voltages and are sold in 3- to 4-foot lengths; connectors are available that allow the installation to expand as needed. Fixtures can be found in an enormous range of decorative styles, ranging from vividly colored Murano glass shades to miniature stage lights.

- **Recessed Lights.** Another popular method of illuminating wall art is with recessed down lights, often called canister lights. These are set flush with the ceiling so there is no visible light fixture or bulb—a definite plus for living rooms with clean architectural lines. Can lights may be fitted with many accessories like baffles, apertures, and shields that let you control the angle, diffusion, and spread of light beams.

- **Strip Lights.** For collections that sit on shelves or in niches, small strip lights installed at the front edge of a shelf or concealed behind some trim along its sides can provide a pleasingly even appearance. Properly locating the light fixtures is important; through experimentation you may find that backlighting is more effective than downlighting your curios.

Finally, when lighting your living-room collections, be aware that different kinds of light bulbs (the pros call them lamps) have different color-rendering properties. Choosing the lamp that's right for your home will depend on several factors, including how much natural light enters the room. If you're consulting with a lighting designer at a showroom, bring the measurements of the room and the artwork you want to display.

FURNITURE ARRANGEMENT

In order for your living room to really live, or your family room to welcome the family, it helps to understand the basics of furniture planning and placement.

Left and below: A large flat-screen TV is a focal point of this contemporary space only when it's in use. The remainder of the time it blends into the sculptural storage wall that puts the emphasis on warm woods and a collection.

COLLECTION CACHET

Objects of a more light-hearted or decorative nature—pottery, toy trains, antique alarm clocks, travel souvenirs, and the like—can add considerably to the visual impact and expressive character of a family room. To keep treasures like these from being mistaken for clutter, group them together in a way that emphasizes a shared trait. All wooden candlesticks, for instance, or all miniature watering cans or eighteenth-century pewter tankards have a greater presence when they're presented as a collection rather than dispersed individually around the room or throughout the home. Sorting items by color, size, material, texture, or subject matter calls attention to their aesthetic strong suits—and by extension, to your unique tastes.

Left: Shop in unpainted furniture stores or check with your local stock cabinetry dealer for pieces like this painted corner hutch.

Below: Use tables and ottomans that offer storage if space is at a premium in your living room.

Choose a focal point for the room, most often the fireplace, an entertainment center, or perhaps a dramatic window view.

Create at least one seating group centered on the focal point.

Remember that occupants of all sizes and shapes will need to be able to move around the room to get to seating. Keep walkways and aisles wide enough to pass through comfortably, without having to turn sideways or move things.

Don't be afraid to try some furniture pieces placed on an angle, away from the wall.

Provide each seat with adequate lighting from a nearby table or floor lamp that can be easily reached and switched on for reading, studying, or crafting. Do not make the mistake of

SMART tip **Game Plan**

Entertaining as they might be, board games present a storage dilemma with their long and deep dimensions. Keep them close by but concealed by sliding them under the couch.

SMARTtip Lighting Test

Use a flashlight to test how light from different angles affects your collection displays. Shine it from above and below, close and from a distance at the objects, noting how each angle impacts their appearance.

relying solely on overhead lighting, which can be harsh and uninviting, and cause shadows. Overhead lighting is really designed to supply ambient light to allow you to move safely about spaces.

Try to provide each seat with a place to set down a beverage, book, or newspaper. A large square or circular coffee table in the center of a furniture grouping can serve as landing space for many of the seats. Or purchase circular, knock-down fiberboard end tables and cover them with fabric tablecloths you buy or make.

Provide a family-sized game table with a lamp. This is the ideal spot for games, coupon clipping, and hobbies like knitting or scrapbooking. If your room seems too small for this, consider a drop-leaf table that folds down when not in use to conserve space.

Above right: This family room is the real gathering spot in the house. Built-in cabinets help to keep it cozy and organized.

Right: In this room, open soffits above the bookcases provide space for oversized items.

Before undertaking a storage makeover, it's a good idea to get acquainted with the nitty-gritty of the room.

ONE Understand the scale of the space. Is it tall, long, and narrow? Or cubic and fairly well balanced in length, depth, and height? Maybe the ceiling is lower than you like, but the other proportions are pleasing. All of these issues will affect the size, shape, and placement of any furniture you use in the room. Are there many doors and windows? If so, that will impose some limits on wall display and storage space, too.

TWO Change or enhance the shape of the space. Keeping your storage situation in mind, decide if you want to try to change the form of the room or enhance it. Shrink a long space by keeping the corners of the room open. Give the illusion of height with shelves that run from floor to ceiling.

Below: Group small prints and paintings on one wall to create the look of one large piece.

SMARTtip In the Best Light

And what about those small tubular picture lights that attach to a painting's frame? Not exactly a curator's first choice: they usually fail to illuminate the artwork uniformly, leaving vertical bands near the borders in shadow.

THREE Select storage pieces. Built-in units or freestanding furniture? Balancing your budget against your schedule will often help lead to a decision on this point. Store-bought shelving is a quick and relatively inexpensive fix, while custom cabinetry requires time and money—but the result will be a one-of-a-kind design that is tailored to your storage needs. Remember: if you're shopping for something to house a collection, measure the objects. Or opt for adjustable shelves you can rearrange.

Opposite: If you collect, you need display space. Here, a pleasing arrangement adds personality to the room.

a gallery of smart ideas

1 Custom cabinets house a wet bar in this large family room.

2 On the other side of the same room, more cabinetry conceals the TV.

3 Wicker cubes inside a fireplace opening look great and stay out of the way.

4 A custom built-in accommodates a large TV among other things.

5 Plan built-in storage to suit the architectural style of the space.

6 Experiment with the objects you want to display until you arrive at a pleasing composition.

7 A vintage oil portrait suitably completes this fireplace wall.

5
6
7

CHAPTER 5

DINING ROOM GATHERINGS

- FREESTANDING CABINETS
- BUILT-IN STORAGE
- ALL FOR SAFEKEEPING

In this era of open kitchens and flexible family rooms, where meals are often served at all hours and on the fly, the traditional dining room has become less important or at least less frequented in many households. With family members coming and going to various organized extracurricular activities and both mom and dad sometimes working late, there's little time and energy or too few family members present to participate in a formal evening meal around the dining room table. And with extended families often living in different cities or an entire continent apart, gone are the days of the multigenerational gatherings in the dining room for a weekly Sunday roast with all the trimmings, including the good china. Yet as lifestyles have changed and the dining room has undergone this seminal shift, its core function still calls for storing and organizing meal service essentials, even if the room is put to use only on holidays or for special family celebrations.

In some households, the dining room is a multifunctional space. Some homeowners prefer to use the dining room partly as an office or a library. Or in a home that does not have a dining room, a corner in another room may be called into service when company comes to dinner. Both scenarios can present special space problems.

SMART tip **Space Saver**

To conserve drawer space, arrange rows of spoons and forks with the tops and bottoms alternating.

Because dining rooms are typically located in the public area of the house, it's important to keep them tidy. If you use yours as a part-time office, reserve space in the breakfront or some other cabinet where you can keep supplies and office equipment peripherals handy but out of sight. Some people think that nothing is as charming and cozy as a library-and-dining-room combination. Bookcases can be used to store and display large serving pieces, and sturdy china cabinets can hold lightweight books or neatly stacked periodicals.

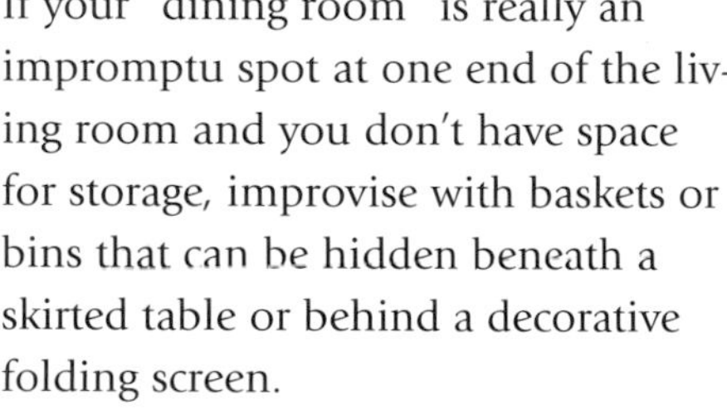

If your "dining room" is really an impromptu spot at one end of the living room and you don't have space for storage, improvise with baskets or bins that can be hidden beneath a skirted table or behind a decorative folding screen.

FREESTANDING CABINETS

You'll find a wide array of freestanding furniture pieces in all styles, from contemporary to traditional and everything in between, that are designed to act as dining room storage and display. When it comes to

Left: An open hutch provides a display of colorful china that adds to the convivial mood of the room's lively decor.

Opposite: An unexpected partnering of practical storage and a dramatic setting injects this dining room-library with rich character.

THE CIVIL WAR
PATHFINDERS
Passages
Velázquez
Valentin SEROV
SARGENT

choosing storage furniture for this room, keep practicality as well as good looks in mind.

When you're shopping for dining-room cabinets, check for quality so that you'll get the most function from whatever pieces you buy. Be sure shelves and drawer slides are sturdy and well supported so that the furniture can hold heavy china as well as fragile objects. Open and close them to see if they handle smoothly. Also, look for adjustable shelves, which offer the most flexibility and make it easy to change the interior configuration if storage needs or display preferences change. It's always wise to take a measuring tape along on shopping trips. If your dinnerware is oversized or if you collect large chargers, platters, or tureens, measure the depth of the shelves to be sure they can accommodate those items.

SMARTtip Cart Tricks

An old-fashioned tea trolley can be invaluable in the dining room. Roll it up to the table to act as a carving station; shuttle it between the kitchen and dining room with dessert and coffee service—its use is only limited by your imagination.

Above: A tall cabinet emphasizes the height of the room, and its glass-fronted doors frame a display for diners.

Opposite : Vintage pieces can be affordable and restyled. This cabinet interior (inset) was painted to match the walls.

SMARTtip Padding Protects

To keep plates from scratching one another, slip a circle of chamois or flannel between each stacked dish.

ADAPTING EXISTING FURNITURE

If new furniture is not in the budget, consider painting or applying a faux-finish technique to an old piece that is still serviceable but dated or unattractive. Paint or refinish a second-hand dresser or bureau to hold table linens and flatware. Play up vintage appeal with a crackle finish, or turn a humble piece of furniture into something elegant with a handsome faux bois (painted wood grain) technique. If a chest is large and sturdy, the drawers can be put to excellent use to store china. Line the interiors with readily available rubber or plastic shelf matting to keep the stacks of dishes from sliding when the drawers are operated.

BUILT-IN STORAGE

If your dining room is odd-shaped, you might consider adding built-in storage to the space. If the room is small, custom-made corner units could be a wise investment. Although it might be costly, the custom option allows you to create made-to-measure storage that includes interiors that are tailored to fit your items. Before making this investment, get estimates from several carpenters. Ask for references (ideally from people you know) and to see examples of similar finished projects. If made-to-order furniture is beyond your means, take a measuring tape along on a visit to an unfinished furniture store. Usually, these outlets sell corner units that you might be able to retrofit into your dining room. Paint or stain them to coordinate with the room's color scheme or the other wood finishes in the room, such as the trim or the table.

Above right: Corner storage cabinets are an economical use of space, especially in small rooms.

Right: Building a buffet into one wall preserves the clean lines of a modern interior.

SMARTtip Step Saver

It may seem intuitive, but if you have one dining-room storage unit that's used primarily for decorative display and one that serves a functional role, try to position the latter piece closer to the kitchen. You'll save steps by not having to walk across the dining room to reach serving pieces and dishes.

Above and right: In space-challenged houses and apartments, creativity is key to storage. The cabinetry in this dining room is home to an assortment of kids' gear and a small audio system that can be hidden behind the doors, plus an array of books, dishes, glasses, and even the family's message center.

Semi-Custom and Stock Cabinetry. You can use semi-custom or stock cabinets and the available interior options to customize your storage. If you choose to do this, think about cabinets that, like ones in the kitchen, extend all the way to the ceiling to eke out more storage space. While you might need a stepladder to reach the highest shelves, the technique makes great use of an otherwise wasted area.

ALL FOR SAFEKEEPING

Even if the space is used only infrequently on special occasions or holidays, many dining rooms are the storage place for treasured family heirlooms that include fine table linens, multiple place settings of dishes, silver or flatware, and numerous stemware and glasses. You may want some of these lovely things on display and others tucked away securely and discreetly. Here are some ideas.

PUTTING AWAY LINENS PROPERLY
Natural-fiber table linens, including cloths and napkins made of cotton, silk, or linen, are susceptible to decay and mold, so they should be stored in a dry place away from light and dust. Left untreated, stains will set while in storage, so put away only freshly laundered and ironed linens. Fold them neatly before putting them in drawers, or hang cloths on wooden hangers. To protect fragile fabrics against yellowing, interleave them with sheets of acid-free tissue paper, available in retail stores, online, or by mail order.

TAKING SUITABLE CARE OF FLATWARE

When storing sterling and silverplate flatware, the objective is twofold: efficient organization, so pieces can be retrieved easily when needed, and protection of the metal finish. The traditional silvercloth-lined wooden chest is fine for most collections; it compactly stores dozens of knives, forks, and spoons while guarding against tarnish. If you own more than one set of silver or if it's a large service for 12 or more persons, you might find it easier to outfit several drawers to house all of the flatware.

There are a couple of ways to do this. If your buffet or sideboard has large shallow drawers, the place settings can be arranged loosely but carefully on a bed of tarnish-inhibiting silvercloth. For an additional barrier, place a blanket of the same cloth on top. Another option, if drawer space is ample, is to use soft grippers that hold individual

To minimize wrinkles, drape table runners and cloths over a padded (preferable) or sturdy wooden hanger before hanging them in the closet or an armoire. For more protection, store them in a garment bag. Cushion the hanger or the rods with a few folded sheets of archival (acid-free) tissue paper to deter creases and to prevent staining the fabric. Don't let the fabric puddle at the bottom, or you'll be doing some last-minute ironing before your dinner party. If you can't hang them, fold them neatly in a shallow acid-free box or wrap them in tissue paper. Another option: launder, but don't iron items until just before using them. Sometimes all you have to do to eliminate minor wrinkles is spritz the cloth with a little cold water and place it the clothes dryer, set on wrinkle-free, for a few minutes.

Opposite: An antique French provincial cabinet has found a second life in this dining room as a compact buffet.

Above: Situated behind the chairs, an integral sideboard helps keep the traffic path around the table open for easy circulation.

Right: Lined in silver cloth, segmented drawers keep cutlery organized and tarnish-free.

utensils securely. Before fixing them in place permanently, it's a wise strategy to map out their intended exact location inside the drawer. Take one place setting and compose it on a sheet of kraft paper that's been trimmed to the interior dimensions of the drawer. When you've devised a successful arrangement, make notations with chalk or a pencil inside the real drawer, and then install the grippers.

STORING CHINA

China is best stored in any of five principle kinds of traditional dining room furniture: the buffet, the breakfront, the china cabinet, the hutch, or the sideboard. Each has distinctive design characteristics. The piece that's right for you depends on the size and style of your dining room, as well as the quantity and quality of the place settings.

Buffet. Sort of a dresser for dishware, the waist-high buffet has a mix of drawers and shelves behind its hinged doors, providing potential storage for everything needed to set a table. This is where larger serving pieces—tureens, platters, chafing dishes, coffee pots—often go, along with smaller odd pieces of china or glass such as vases and dishes for candy or crudités.

Breakfront. The breakfront is another versatile piece of furniture that combines concealed storage with display space. A breakfront may be a combination of drawers, closed cupboards, and shelves. It's distinguishing design feature is a protruding center section.

When filling up a breakfront with your treasures, remember that the most convenient storage falls between your knee and your shoulder, so plan to store the heaviest and the most frequently used items, such as massive platters and other large serving pieces, in this spot.

Left: Massing objects that share similar shapes and colors is a basic principle of the art of display.

Left: A pair of built-in cabinets define the doorway to this dining room. Light and bright, they can hold all the settings and serviceware for the largest family feast.

HOUSING FOR GLASSWARE AND CRYSTAL

Glass and crystal are often displayed alongside the most attractive china, but there are more specialized and secure ways of storing them. One is within a bar cart or cocktail cabinet. In addition to racks and shelves for stemware, these pieces typically come with compartments and niches that organize all of the paraphernalia that threaten to overwhelm a refined beverage service—an ice bucket and tongs, coasters, a cutting board, paring knife, measuring jiggers, and cocktail shakers. Still squeezed for space? Put the underside of a shelf to work with a wire rack that holds inverted wine glasses or any other kind of stemware by their bases.

Before you begin rearranging the contents of your dining room, use the Smart Steps on the next page to make your work more efficient and the results close to perfection.

China Cabinet. The china cabinet serves as the showcase for your tabletop treasures. Tall, with glass doors and shelves that let light penetrate throughout the interior, the china cabinet is designed specifically for housing and displaying collections such as tea sets and delicate figurines. For smaller dining rooms, a scaled-down chest with an attached hutch or simply a wall hutch or dish rack may provide suitable storage and display space.

Sideboard. Standing on elegant slim legs, the long and relatively narrow sideboard is similar in proportion to a console table but has drawers for silverware and other flat articles. Some designs feature a pair of small, lockable cupboards (for valuables, such as sterling pieces) that are ideal for small serving dishes and trays.

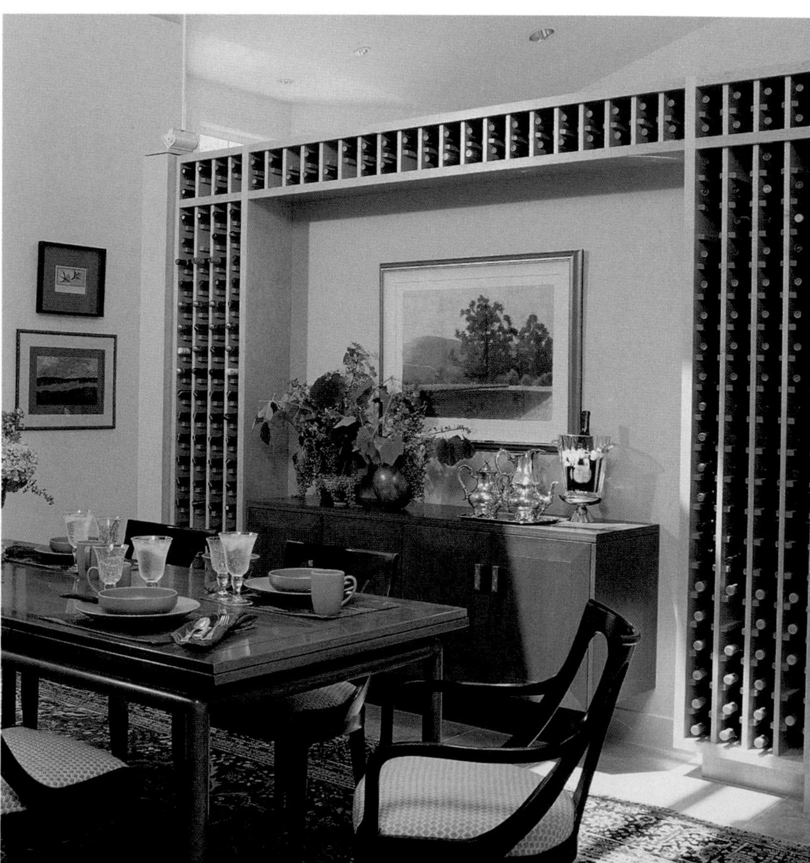

Right: A custom-built wine rack creates an alcove that frames the freestanding sideboard in this dining room.

SMART steps

ONE Cull the collection. Throw out chipped or cracked china or glass. Repeat the procedure for stained tablecloths and napkin or placemat sets that are incomplete, out of fashion, faded, or worn. Not only will this free up more storage space, but with the damaged goods out of the picture you will be able to assess your replacement and storage needs with accuracy.

TWO Store it clean and at the ready. Rather than wait for the night before the family feast, make it a rainy day activity to polish the silverware and wash and press the napery. Remember: silver must be completely dry before it can be put away.

THREE Categorize. Keep your china together by pattern (if you have more than one). Separate serving pieces from place settings. Then within each pattern, sort by size: all dinner plates, all salad plates, dessert plates, soup bowls or coupes, cups, mugs, and saucers. Do the same with your silverware, stemware, and glasses.

FOUR Count what's on hand. Draw up a list of how many of each piece you have. Then use it as the basis for making or buying the correct number of appropriately sized storage accessories.

SMART tip — Wrap It

For long-term storage, clean, dry flatware can be wrapped tightly in plastic to keep tarnish at bay.

Above left: Choose storage pieces that complement the style of the space. Here, a rustic hutch is the focus of a countrified dining room.

Above: Built-in cabinets add architectural elegance and order to this combined dining room and library. Open shelves on top display books, and closed cabinets on the bottom store dinnerware and serving pieces.

Right: Fresh color and a mixture of styles puts an eclectic spin on this small but personality-packed room.

B
Oh what a beautiful day.
PARIS

CHAPTER 6

RETHINKING BEDROOM STORAGE

- THE BED SPACE
- CHESTS AND NIGHTSTANDS
- CLOSETS
- MORE ROOM, MORE STORAGE

Ideally, your bedroom should be your personal sanctuary—a serene private place where you can sleep well and become refreshed and revived to greet another crazy day. But that can't be the case if the room is so cluttered that you can't find the bed, or the floor is knee-deep in heaps of clothing, week-old newspapers, or back issues of magazines. If you long to create the kind of bedroom atmosphere that allows you to begin each day calmly, without a frantic hunt for that other black shoe or your navy suit jacket, it's important to provide the means to maintain order.

But what if it's not the jumble in your room that brings on an anxiety attack? What if it's your youngster's—or worse, your teenager's—pile of rubble that causes the alarm? Talk to your kids and offer to help sort through the piles of clothes, CDs, or old toys. Tell them to get rid of items that they don't wear or want anymore. Suggest selling unwanted items in a resale shop or online. The extra cash can be an incentive to clean up their act. Once that's accomplished, you can segue into methods for keeping the room neat and for properly putting away their things. Show them by example. You can do this with confidence once you've followed the advice in this chapter, which explains how to create harmony and order in a bedroom—even a teeny one.

In addition to a comfortable bed, the basics include at least one nightstand, some type of drawer storage for folded garments, hanging space for clothing, and possibly storage for out-of-season clothes. If the bedroom belongs to a child or teenager, add toy and game storage and possibly a spot to do homework or keep school papers and projects organized. Don't forget about computer gear.

THE BED SPACE

A bed often takes up a lot of space, but it doesn't have to hamper the storage quotient of the room. The familiar mattress and box spring affixed to a wooden or metal frame offers little in the way of storage options, but you can do what practically everybody does: stash things under the bed, which is not always a bad idea when you package or box the items properly. However, there are a number of bed types other than the traditional that either incorporate storage compartments in their design or free up space in the room.

Platform Bed. Also known as a captain's bed, this type of bed features a mattress that rests on a platform, which is over a bank of drawers. The drawers can open on one or both sides of the bed and, depending on their depth, can be used for anything from clothes to sporting equipment.

SMART tip Lights On

Even the best-organized closet is of little use if you can't see the contents. Light up the interior with illuminated hanging rods, door-activated overhead lights, or an old-fashioned pull-cord ceiling fixture.

Loft Bed. A design more suitable for adults, older kids, or teens, the loft bed is similar to a bunk bed, but without the lower berth. The elevated bed is supported by pillars of shelving, drawers, and often a built-in desk or work area, making it a storage superpower.

Opposite: The platform bed, with its integral drawers, makes great use of space that otherwise houses nothing but forgotten slippers and dust bunnies.

Left: An elegant yet casual look that's full of personality: his and her night tables, storage chests, and a pair of chairs.

Above: The loft bed maximizes usable space in a small area for kids who must share a room.

ANNE SEXTON
HAMMETT
Lillian Hellman
THE BUNKER
SUPERNATURAL

Left and below: This classic Murphy bed folds neatly into traditional white painted cabinetry, thereby freeing floor space for other uses during the day.

Murphy Bed. Familiar to dwellers of cramped studio apartments, the classic Murphy bed can also play a useful role in the suburban home. Installing one of these pull-down, fold-up units in a rarely occupied guest bedroom allows the space to be more productive in the everyday patterns of family life. For example, with the bed up and out of the way, the room could be used for yoga or exercise, for crafts, or as a home office. An ingenious variation that's part Murphy, part sleeper couch is a foldout bed that's hidden in the base of a built-in window seat.

CONSIDERING OTHER OPTIONS

Another way to eke out additional storage from near the the bed is to transform the headboard into a collection of niches and shelves. No matter if it's bought, built, or cribbed together using a pair of bookcases, this design is an efficient and easy way to organize the assorted reading material, glasses, and papers that gravitate to the bedside.

Opposite: If you make a habit of going to bed with a good book—or if the guest room doubles as a library—a headboard designed with shelves for your favorites is a practical idea. Include a reading lamp with an articulated arm.

Below: Stash out-of-season items behind doors on the higher shelves, and put everyday items where kids can reach them or put them away easily.

SMART tip Sort It Out

Keep a laundry bag or basket in each bedroom. It simplifies returning clean clothes to their rightful owner.

Under-bed Boxes. Regardless of whether you choose prefabricated plastic containers or construct the boxes out of plywood, use lids to keep the dust bunnies at bay. If you want to squeeze even more space out from under the bed, consider bed risers (usually available at bed and bath stores), which boost the height of the frame by a few inches, allowing for taller containers. In any case, make sure to measure both the outline of the bed and the clearance between the frame and the floor before purchasing underbed storage boxes to guarantee they will fit completely underneath.

Above: A variety of pieces provides options: shelves display favorites; an armoire hides clothes; and a small chest of drawers doubles as a nightstand.

Below: The secret to a serene bedroom space: begin with a soothing, simple palette and plenty of storage to keep clutter at bay.

CHESTS AND NIGHTSTANDS

Even if the bed you select offers some provision for storage, most people agree: you can never have too many closets—or drawers. Furniture intended for storage, such as tall bureaus, chests of drawers, and nightstands are called *casegoods* by the furniture industry. (Armoires also fall into this category, but they will be discussed later in this chapter.) If you're feeling the crunch, maybe the problem isn't a lack of drawer storage, but the chaos inside the drawers that's taking up space.

MAXIMIZING DRAWERS

It should go without saying that neatly folded clothes require less space. For a few minutes of time spent folding, you'll save hours at the ironing board, and never be vexed by mismatched socks again. To make room in crowded drawers and keep clothing wrinkle free, learn to fold items properly.

T-shirts. Lay T-shirts face down on the bed or a clean table. Smooth out any wrinkles. Fold over each sleeve. Then fold each side of the shirt to the middle. Flatten the folds. Next, from the bottom, fold the shirt up almost halfway; flatten the fold. Finally, fold one more time to the top, flattening the final fold.

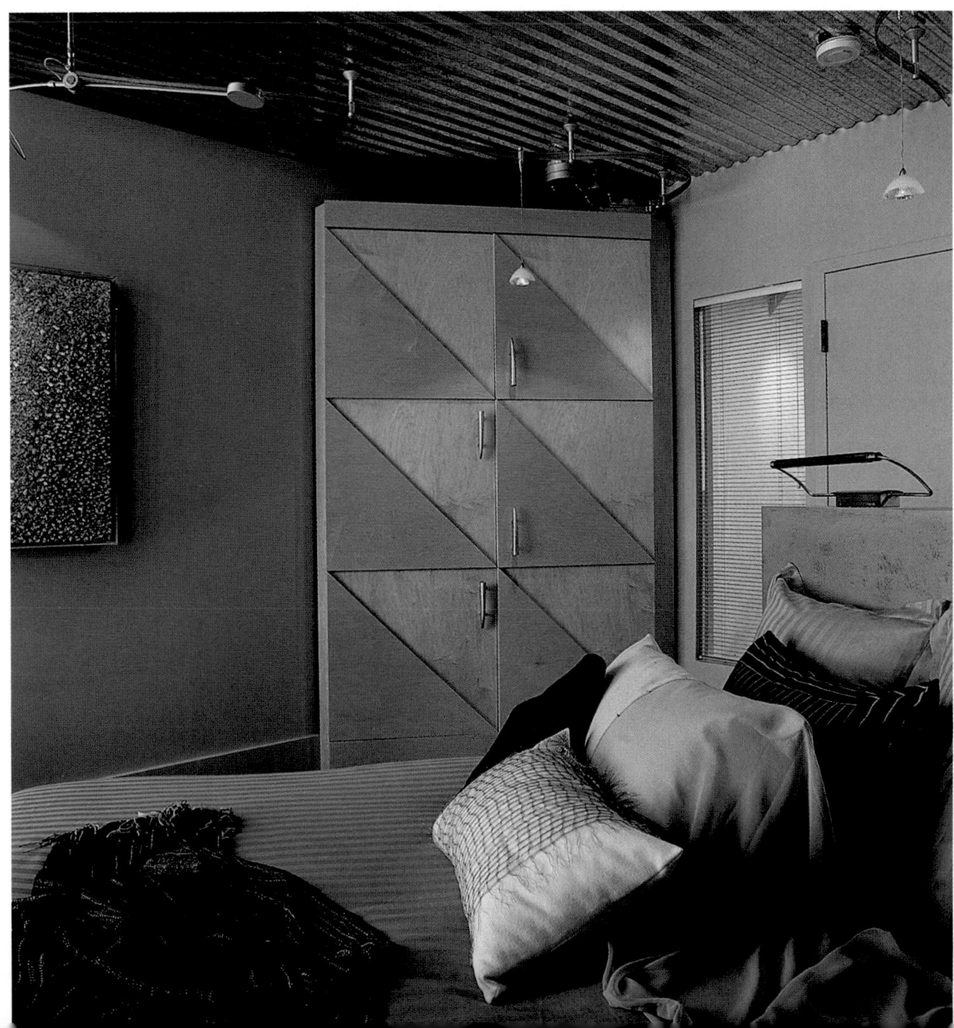

Above right: **Bedrooms with high ceilings can handle tall pieces. If you live with kids, bolt tall furniture to the walls for safety.**

Right: **This custom-made piece fits neatly into the corner.**

SMART tip — Measure Up

To help you plan the optimally functioning clothes closet, here are the standard lengths (in inches, measured from the pole) for hanging everyday garments. If you are taller than average, be sure to raise the pole a bit higher so that garments won't graze the floor.

Men's Clothing	
Pants, folded	32
Pants, unfolded	48
Shirt	38
Suit	40
Ties, folded	32
Topcoat	56
Winter coat	55

Women's Clothing	
Bathrobe	52
Blouse	36
Dress	58
Evening gown	69
Skirt	35
Suit	37
Winter coat	52

Sweaters. Like T-shirts, sweaters should be folded face down. (If the sweater has buttons, fasten them.) Smooth out wrinkles; fold over one side, then the other, followed by the sleeves, positioning them vertically—not across—the back of the sweater. From the bottom, fold up halfway, then once again to just below the collar. Be sure to smooth and flatten each fold as you go.

Button-Down Shirts. Shirts belong on a hanger, but if you must fold and stack them, follow the directions for folding sweaters (above).

Slacks. Dress slacks always belong on a hanger, but sweat pants, pajama bottoms, and heavy jeans or cords are fine for folding. Match the inside seam of each leg; hold them together at the cuff; then bring in both outside seams until the two legs are together and parallel. Smooth down the natural crease in the legs; fold up once to about the knee; and fold again to just below the waist.

Underwear and Socks. Generally, underwear is lightweight and can be left unfolded. However, some people prefer to fold it into a neat square before putting it in a drawer. Socks are best paired and rolled. Match them one on top of the other and parallel. Roll them together, starting at the toes to just below the top of the ankle. Roll the outer sock's cuff over the rest of the ball. If you're really a neat freak, install drawer organizers to separate colors.

Using Drawer Organizers and Inserts. There are also devices that can stretch drawer storage—or at least cut back on the clutter. Crafted of smooth plastic, laminated paper, or wood veneer that won't snag delicate fabrics, drawer inserts or "cubbies" are available in myriad configurations. Modeled after cutlery dividers in kitchen drawers, they keep socks together, neckties neatly rolled, and lingerie tangle-free; the concept is practically foolproof. Other multipurpose dividers can keep stacked shirts or sweaters separated and in place, even when you remove an item.

SMART tip — Double Duty

One sure way to address clutter issues in the bedroom is to have every element serve a storage function. For example, instead of using a table as a nightstand to simply hold a lamp, telephone, and possibly a clock radio, select a small bureau with drawers or doors with shelves to stash bedside reading material or an extra blanket.

TIDYING DRESSER TOPS

Remember, the bedroom is intended as a place of repose, so it should be visually soothing. Don't crowd the tops of dressers and nightstands with too much stuff. If you want to create a display, keep it simple. Try decorative containment: for items that you want handy but hidden, invest in finished boxes that are attractive and practical at the same time. Shop for a variety of sizes in a style or color that reflects the room's decor. These boxes are widely available covered in paper or fabric. You may also find them made of leather, glass, wood, or even plastic. They come in so many styles and sizes that you are sure to find ones that are compatible with your taste. Also, don't forget the timeless change tray for the nightstand, too. It still collects keys and coins as efficiently as it did in your dad's day.

Hutches and Shelves. If the surface of your dresser has already reached its maxi-

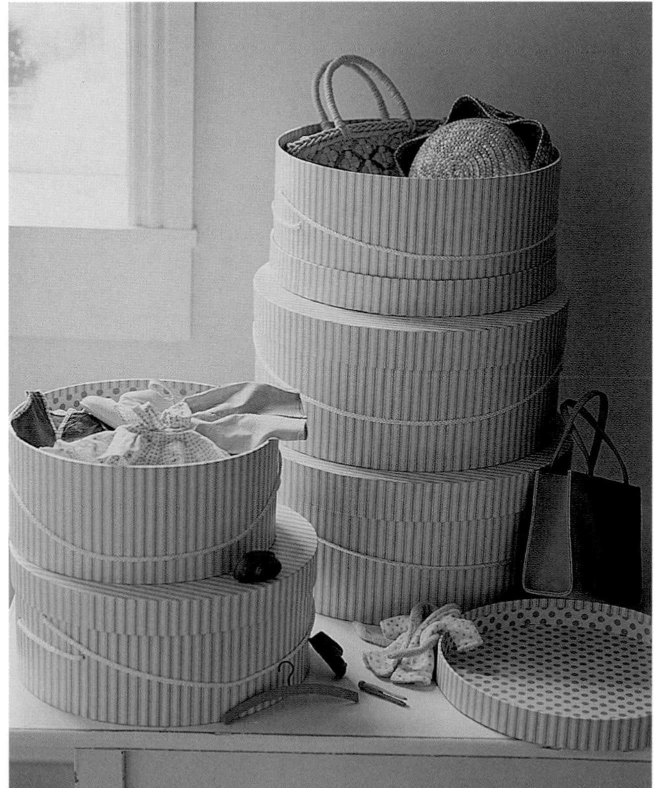

Above right: Collectors might want to showcase items in the bedroom. But remember that only frequent dusting maintains the charm and good looks of objects on display.

Right: A stack or two of decorative boxes that match the room can cleverly conceal an infinite variety of small items.

SMART tip Personal Valet

If what you really long for is a personal dresser to oversee your wardrobe but find it's not in the budget this year, try this instead: scout antique shops, flea markets, or home-wares Web sites, catalogs, or stores for a valet stand or a clothing butler. That's a wooden floor rack that takes up the space of a chair where you can properly hang a man's or woman's suit. The butler usually includes a tray to collect keys and pocket change and acts as a mini dressing room.

Above: Create hidden storage under a vanity by stashing wire drawer units under a utility table top that's skirted with a few yards of pretty fabric. No sewing is required.

Opposite bottom and top: Affix loop-and-hook tape to the tabletop edges and the back of the fabric, and press them together. For access, pull the fabric free.

mum load, think about adding a hutch to it. Make sure that it's in proportion to the dresser. If you purchase an unfinished piece, you can try to match the stain or color with the dresser's, or you can choose a contrasting or complementary finish. Integrate a mirror with a tall design, or keep the hutch short to work with a chest that's long and low.

Another way of addressing dresser overflow is with shelving. Installed on the wall behind the chest, standard shelves are too deep (typically 8 inches) to be of practical use when you're standing in front of the dresser. A better idea is to use a series of shallow ledges (about 4 or 5 inches deep) that can alleviate clutter by holding framed photos, small jewelry, or perhaps a collection of items that lend themselves to display in the bedroom, such as perfume bottles.

Linen Closet Basics

- Label the shelves in the linen closet—"twin sheets" or "bath towels," for example—so that everyone who uses it knows exactly where each item belongs.
- If you stack towels and sheets with the fold facing the front of the linen closet, these items are easier to grab. The closet looks neater, too.
- Keep complete sets of bedding together—pillowcases folded around both top and bottom sheets—to quicken the process of changing the sheets.
- When not in use, comforters and duvets (cleaned, folded neatly, and bagged with a cedar sachet) should occupy the topmost shelves of the linen closet, leaving everyday linens and towels to the shelves that are within easy reach.

CLOSETS

The bedroom closet holds a substantial part of everyone's wardrobe—and in all likelihood a good deal more. Even if your closet is in critical condition— it's virtually impossible to slide hangers easily along the rod, for example—there are ways to improve its usefulness without breaking the bank or your back.

MAXIMIZING HANGING SPACE

You can double or even triple the closet's hanging space by installing additional rods at heights that are sized to suspend clothes such as skirts, blouses, shirts, jackets, folded trousers, and other shorter items. Don't enter into this undertaking without the proper preparation. Especially if you've never planned a fitted closet before, guesstimating is not good enough; once you have thoroughly culled your wardrobe, categorize, count, and measure the length of the garments you'll be storing. To determine the position of the rods, you need to know both the linear feet as well as the hanging length(s) of your complete wardrobe.

A full-service closet needs to provide more than well-orchestrated hanging space. Shoes, bags, sweaters, and accessories need to be stowed, too. Once again, take an unflinching inventory of these items (perhaps it's finally time to say goodbye to those Minnie Mouse platform

Below: Closet organizing systems can be arranged to accommodate any wardrobe, with single- and double-hanging poles, open shelves, and drawer space for folded garments.

shoes?) and measure the keepers. When you're ready to devise your closet's configuration, you have a choice: take the measurements to an organizational consultant (whose services are often included in the price of closet systems purchased from home-storage retailers); or head to your home workshop.

Closet-Stretching Accessories. Shelves for folded garments can run the full height of the closet, or if you don't require that much flat storage, place them around chest height for optimal accessibility. Shoes and boots can go in cubbies or see-through plastic boxes along the floor. Angling the bottom shelf can give you a better view of its holdings. Or look for specially designed racks or fabric pockets to hold several pairs of shoes. Hats and purses, bagged or boxed against dust and scuffs, find a home in the upper shelves of the closet.

Left: A well-planned and well-lit dressing room is the ultimate in bedroom storage convenience.

Above: Individual cubbies keep shoes off the floor, in view, and easy to find at a glance.

Closet Doors

Believe it or not, the kind of door or doors on a reach-in closet can have an impact on the quantity and quality of your storage. A standard hinged door can act like an auxiliary wall surface; both its front and back sides can be fitted with hooks or hanging pouches or pockets that can be stuffed with socks, scarves, and other small accessories. A hinged door poses one drawback for small bedrooms: its outward swing eats into the open space in the room. If that's an issue for you, consider installing either a bifold door or an accordion-style design. Both of these configurations permit the complete contents of the closet to be fully exposed, but the doors—because of their opening mechanism and relatively small surface area—do not lend themselves to being the basis for supplemental storage as a hinged door does. A set of by-pass or sliding doors also solves the swing-space problem, but these can only be installed as a set of two or more, making them suitable for closets with openings that are wider than 3 feet. A pair of side-hinged doors can also be employed in this situation.

An encouraging word to the frugal, or to the footloose: these specialized features don't have to be permanent constructions. Once the rods are installed at the proper heights, you can add relatively inexpensive fabric or wire versions of these custom elements to the basic structure. Of course, if your residential roots are well planted, you might want to make an investment in a closet crafted of fine woods.

Above and right: Providing children with simple and accessible storage is the first step in helping them learn to keep spaces clutter free. A shoe bag with large pockets and bins with handles meet the criteria of "easy-to use."

MORE ROOM, MORE STORAGE

As with most storage, there are alternatives—both large and small—to the conventional reach-in bedroom clothes closet. Some of these take the form of built-in designs, while others are freestanding models. Two examples of the former category are dressing rooms and walk-in closets.

ORGANIZING THE DRESSING ROOM

For many individuals—Beau Brummel fashionistas and regular people alike—the dressing room is the supreme achievement in wardrobe storage. Having a space that's wholly separate from the bedroom not only allows one's sartorial indulgences to be maintained in peak organizational form but preserves the serene atmosphere of the bedroom, as well.

A dressing room should be lined with reach-in closets, cabinets, and casegoods of varying dimensions. A table or central island can hold grooming supplies or act as additional storage. For comfort's sake, you'll want a minimum of 50 square feet of space to accommodate the various forms of storage in the space while allowing for clearance to walk around and change clothes without being hemmed in. You might be able to find this kind of space in a large master bedroom along an outside wall—which would also provide the opportunity to incorporate the requisite window or two into the dressing room. Another possibility that could prove particularly fruitful: combine two existing closets into one luxuriant space. If there is an attic or crawl space over-

Above: A spacious dressing room organizes an entire wardrobe. For true comfort, include seating.

head, have an architect explore the feasibility of expanding the dressing room upwards; even raising the ceiling a foot can add appreciable shelf space.

CREATING A WALK-IN CLOSET

A walk-in closet should measure at least 5 x 7 feet. This will allow room for storage along two walls and still leave enough of a path into the space to survey its complete contents. Unlike a dressing room, where clothing is concealed and protected behind closed doors, everything hanging in a walk-in closet is visible at one time, making the design very efficient. Walk-in closets, like reach-in styles, can be fitted out with tiered hanging rods, drawers and cubbies, shelves, racks, and trays to put every last inch of space to work.

SMARTtip On the Door

The backside of a closet door offers a swath of underutilized space. Consider adding a full-length mirror or racks for ties, belts, or scarves.

INCORPORATING A FREESTANDING CLOSET

The freestanding counterparts to these integrated closet designs are stand-alone furniture and add-on installations. The trusty armoire (the original use of which was as a storage locker for rifles and other arms) is easily repurposed as a wardrobe; just add a rod, perhaps a shelf at the bottom of the unit, and hooks or racks on the inside of the doors and you're set to go. And don't forget about using the top of the armoire as another shelf; a basket with a lid to keep out dust, or a box or two, will keep things up there in good order.

Closet Lighting. Closets of all sizes and configurations need to be properly lit. After all, what good is an organized wardrobe if you can't see what you're looking for? In reach-in designs, it's handy (or rather, hands-free) to install a ceiling light that automatically turns on when the door is opened and turns off when it's closed. (As a fire safety precaution be sure any light fixture you install can not come into direct contact with stored items.) Depending on the size of space, more than one wall-switched fixture may be needed to illuminate walk-in closets and dressing rooms; in the latter, adding a sensitively scaled table lamp on top of a built-in chest of drawers can inject the space with a person-

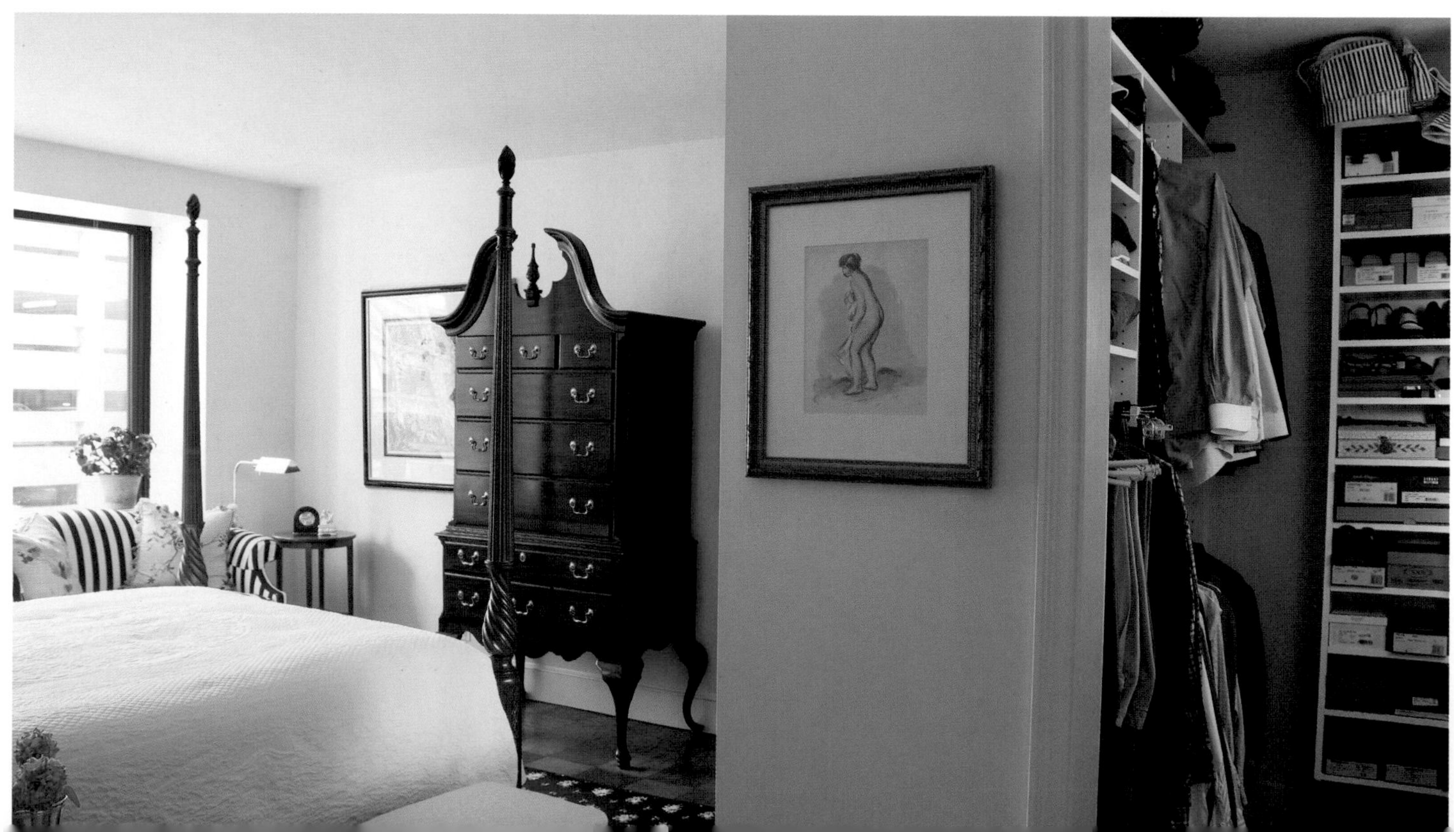

SMARTtip Guest Space

In a makeshift guest room during the holidays or whenever temporary clothing storage arrangements are needed, a bare-bones rolling garment rack can be dressed up by tenting it in a fabric that coordinates with the room's interior design scheme and color palette. Should you run short of time or talent as far as needlework is concerned, look around for prefinished drapery panels that, with a strategic tuck here and pin there, could be used to drape the rack. While not a permanent solution, it's certainly better than a naked hanging rod —both aesthetically and when it comes to protecting clothes from dust.

alized touch. Thinking along that line, don't feel compelled to use ho-hum fluorescent fixtures in the closet. Be adventurous and add a little character to the space—imagine how a petite chandelier would add sparkle or a simple Shaker-inspired pendant might appear. If hardwiring the lights in the closet isn't doable, compact corded or even battery-powered designs can

Opposite: A small effort—and organized containment—can keep items in a doorless walk-in closet attractively arranged yet within easy reach.

Right: Look for freestanding furniture that features adjustable shelves that can be arranged to suit your personal storage requirements.

SMART tip **Use It or Lose It**

If you haven't worn something in a year, take it out of your closet and donate it to charity.

bring a bit of brightness to the space. Small clamp-on lamps can be focused to wash against the wall or bounce light off the ceiling, and tiny spotlights with flexible goosenecks can be directed to aim light right where it's needed most. New additions to the scene are hanging rods that have sections that actually light up.

Now that you know what you need, are you still looking for ways to get started? Follow these Smart Steps; then get to work!

ONE Apropos of the bedroom, dream. What do you need—and wish—to get out of your bedroom storage? Nearly every scheme includes purely pragmatic hanging space, but now's the time to fantasize. Would life be perfect if you could see every pocketbook in your collection all at once? Would dedicated sock drawers send you (or your spouse) to nirvana? Maybe you've always wanted to shelve your sweaters in the closet rather than the dresser.

TWO Scrapbook. Go through magazines, catalogs, and books, and tear out or copy photos of closets that inspire you. Take notes on what you like about each installation; then make a master list of amenities. Consider appearances: do dark woods appeal, or light-colored, low-maintenance laminates? Should the door (or doors) be hinged or sliding? Solid or louvered? Do you like basket-type drawers or are you partial to the conventional box-style? Then think about the functional features that have caught your attention. From dressing tables and full-length mirrors, specialized racks for shoe storage, segmented trays for rolled ties, and more, the list of closet-storage options and add-ons is a long one.

THREE Make it happen. With your vision of a perfect closet having taken shape, it's time to see how well it meshes with what's on the market. You can work with an architect or designer and create a one-of-a-kind wardrobe that's been tailored just for you. Semicustom systems offer a menu of prefabricated components that are assembled to fit an existing closet. Available through specialized storage retailers as well as from closet-organizer franchises, they are affordable and flexible. Then there's the do-it-yourself approach, often taking the form of basic kits of coated-wire rods and shelves.

Opposite: Frosted-glass doors look slick and camouflage the contents of a pair of clothes armoires that are built into this space-saving bed system.

Above: A walk-in closet requires adequate lighting for choosing clothing and locating items that may be stored in the far corners.

1
2
3
4
prince
EXTENDER

a gallery of...

1&2 It's the ultimate in TV storage for the bedroom: a pop-up cabinet located at the foot of the bed.

3 Use shoe pockets imaginatively. They can corral a variety of small items such as school supplies, scarves, and toys.

4 Under-bed drawer storage is suitable for any age and for many items.

5 & 6 Every little girl's room must house the inevitable stuffed-animal and treasured trinket collection. Here shelves surround the window and showcase these special objects, keeping them out of the way and tidy.

7 A playful platform bed and play area incorporates drawers for stashing toys out of sight.

7

1

2

3

...smart ideas

1 A wall of custom-designed built-ins includes floor-to-ceiling closets.

2 Natural light brightens a dressing room. But be sure clothing doesn't hang in direct sunlight.

3 While it's not advisable to turn your bedroom into a home office, it is acceptable to integrate one into the guest room. Be sure you include closed storage so important documents are not on display when guests use the space.

4 In a small bedroom, consider adding space-stretching custom-made built-ins. Or use stock cabinetry combined to create personalized storage.

5 Light wood tones prevent these armoires from overpowering the room.

6 Manufacturers of kitchen cabinetry make units suitable for bedroom storage, too.

C H A P T E R 7

ORGANIZING THE BATHROOM

- HOW TO MAKE ANY BATH "BIGGER"
- A PLAN FOR MASTER BATHS
- FAMILY-FITTING IDEAS

Of all the spaces within the home, the bathroom presents one of the most interesting storage design challenges. It's typically the smallest room of the house, particularly in an older home, yet it's multifunctional status and shared usage make good organization and the absence of clutter an imperative. Besides serving bathing, toileting, and grooming needs, each bathroom in your home should provide a place for fresh towels as well as a spot to hang used ones until they dry. Some families like to include at least one hamper for linens and another for soiled clothing. And then there's containment for the assortment of grooming supplies and appliances that can clutter the vanity if there's no place to put them other than on the countertop or, worse, the toilet tank. It's always practical to keep a few extra rolls of toilet tissue handy, too, but not on the floor next to the toilet. What about the cleaning bucket, cleansers, and perhaps even a plunger? Yes, you may want to find a place for them, too.

When it comes to soaps and shampoos, remember that it's not a good idea to store anything on the ledge of the bathtub. While convenience, and sometimes expediency, are demanded of the bath, safety should also be a prime consideration. On top of all this, the rigorous use of the room calls for durable, easy-to-clean surfaces and finishes. Many of these divergent needs can be met by intelligently designed, well-planned storage.

HOW TO MAKE ANY BATH "BIGGER"

If your house is at least 50 years old and hasn't been expanded, chances are there's only one bathroom and it's small. Bathrooms of this era are typically 5x7 feet. However, vertical storage can respond effectively to tight-squeeze situations. Affordable floor-to-ceiling pole systems with trays, racks, and mirrors can be stacked in various combinations. If you're not familiar with this concept, think back to your last visit to the dentist: tools and implements are kept on trays that can be swiveled back and forth as needed.

Look to the back of the door as an upright storage zone, too. But because the area behind the door typically doesn't have much air circulation, it's not the best spot to hang wet towels; they won't get a chance to dry thoroughly. Consider installing a fabric or vinyl shoe storage panel there instead, and stuff its pockets with curlers, cotton balls, and other sundries.

SMART tip More & More

Stacking two or even three medicine cabinets not only stretches storage, but it also creates a full-length mirror in the bathroom.

Another place that lends itself to vertical storage is the wall behind the commode. Install shallow shelves or a cupboard there. Just make sure that anything you hang above the toilet is no deeper than the toilet tank. Don't forget to allow for head clearance, too—a floor-standing storage unit should have shelves that can be adjusted to suit everyone who uses the room.

GARAGE THE GEAR

The dense tangle of twisted cords on hair dryers, shavers, electric toothbrushes, and other small appliances not only looks messy but can be dangerous, too. One solution to this problem borrows from the kitchen: an appliance garage. Built into the vanity, this cabinet can corral corded grooming devices, keeping them out of sight but within reach. Enclose the garage with a hinged, swing-out door that coordinates with the cabinetry in the room or, if counter space is tight, use a slide-up tambour design. Refer to your local building code to see whether it's permissible to locate electrical outlets inside the cabinet.

Tilt-out Panel. Another storage idea imported from the kitchen is the tilt-out tray, which is created from the vanity's false-drawer panel in front of the sink. Used in the kitchen to keep sponges and scrubbers from straying, you'll find it's handy for storing combs and brushes or small clips and hairpins in the bathroom.

Opposite top: A custom design of open and closed storage plays up rectangular shapes in this contemporary bath.

Opposite bottom; left and right: A painted wood unit (left) and shelves built into the wall (right) offer two solutions.

Above: A tambour door conceals storage for small grooming appliances.

SMART tip — Conceal Clutter

If your bath has a wall-hung sink, a console basin, a pedestal sink, or any other design that doesn't allow for a vanity cabinet, consider hanging a skirt of fabric around its base that reaches down to the floor. Attaching it to the bottom edge of the sink with lengths of hook-and-loop tape allows it to be removed for washing. Place a small shelf unit or trolley cart behind the curtain to hold bathroom essentials.

SMARTtip On the Wall

Keep toothbrushes off the countertop by installing a ceramic organizer on the wall that matches the tile.

Creative Containers. There are dozens of small cosmetic and grooming articles used in the bath on a daily basis. If they are left untamed, they will quickly subsume any sense of order. Organizing these items can be improvised—collect cotton balls or swabs in a pretty coffee mug; stash small brushes and applicators in spice jars, a miniature flower pot, or even an egg cup. Such an ad hoc approach lends loads of character and charm to what can be a sterile storage situation, and it's especially appropriate in a cottage or country decor. Of course, in a bath that has a more contemporary feel, sleek acrylic boxes and trays will supply the same structure in a far more stylistically compatible way.

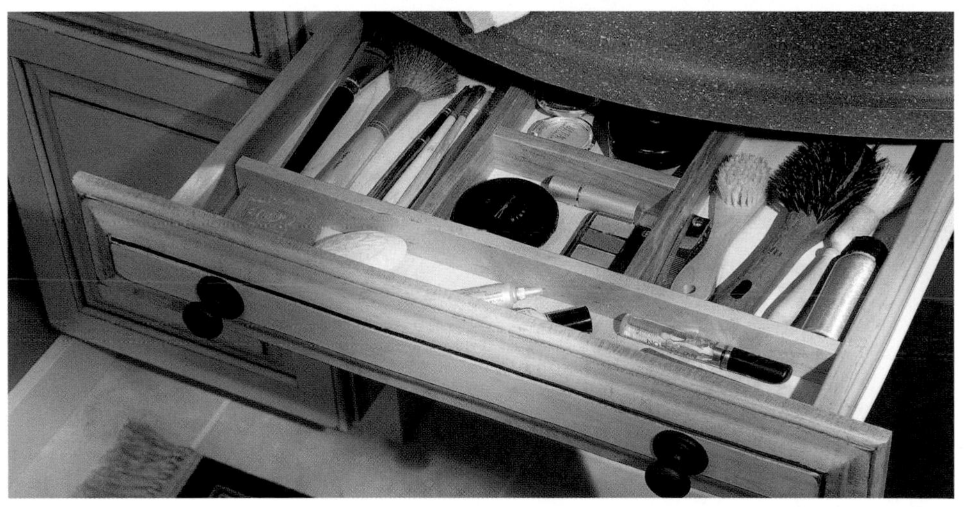

Shelving Selections. Goods stored out in the open on shelves or in cubbies will be subjected to the damp, warm atmosphere of the bathroom every day. If these items aren't in frequent use, perforated shelving can help deter mildew from forming. In general, stay away from materials that are prone to delaminate or rust. (Make sure glass is tempered and has no sharp edges.) Among the wood types that hold up to moisture are teak, ash, cherry, and maple. (But don't forget the importance of a venting system.)

Opposite: A portable rolling cart keeps toiletries and bath supplies close at hand.

Top: Attach shelves to the inside of vanity cabinet doors to help stretch storage space.

Above right: Drawer inserts keep grooming supplies neat and orderly.

Right: Rollouts bring the contents of cabinets forward so smaller items are easy to locate.

BUILT-IN STORAGE

An emerging trend in built-in storage in the bath puts a bank of cabinets and shelves or cubbyholes at one or both ends of the tub. To protect their contents from splashes, they are usually situated at waist or counter height and often moved back away from the rim of the tub.

Shower Storage. Provisions inside the shower stall are important not only from an organizational standpoint, but from a safety vantage as well. If loose bottles, soaps, or toys get underfoot, you can slip and suffer a serious injury. Storage niches built into the walls should be shallow and designed so that they don't collect water; the bottom of a niche should slope slightly to facilitate drainage. Consider placing one at a level that's within a child's reach. As an alternative, a caddy that slips over the showerhead is economical and can be updated easily to reflect changes in decor.

To eliminate clutter and find more storage in your bathroom—whatever its size and no matter how many people use it—ponder the Smart Steps on the next page.

Above: Don't waste space. Build shelves into the wall at the end of the tub.

Right: A tall narrow cabinet fits neatly between this sink and tub and greatly improves bathroom organization.

Opposite top: Basket drawers built into an extension of the tub deck and surround provide a place for a few extra towels.

Opposite bottom: In some cases, shelves can be installed on the wall next to the tub.

SMART steps

ONE **Consider who uses the room.** Is it just one person or several—a single guy or gal, an elderly person, toddlers, someone who uses a wheelchair, or mom, dad, and the kids? Each of them has different expectations and experiences of the room.

TWO **Think about patterns, needs, and habits.** Some folks are in and out in a jiffy: morning shower, shave, and they're away. Others primp, sometimes seemingly around the clock. Daily health-care procedures can be important for many people. Toilet training for little ones requires frequent visits of varying duration. Identifying all the various tasks performed in your bathroom will underscore specific storage needs that might otherwise have gone unnoticed.

THREE **Be realistic about your options and how they can enhance your lifestyle.** Open shelves could make access for seniors easier. For the budding cosmetologist (or a typical teenage girl), cabinets and drawers in a variety of sizes will facilitate storing items as diverse as curling irons, makeup in its myriad forms, and blow dryers. That bubble bath hedonist will sigh over tubside cubbies designed to hold cushy turkish towels and spa lotions and potions. The idea is to let bathroom storage be the bridge between people and purpose.

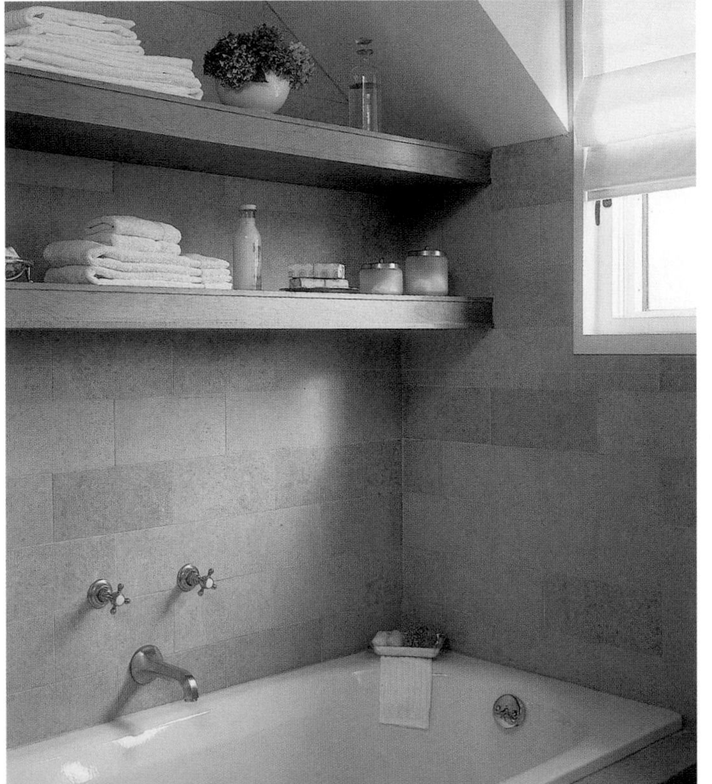

SMART tip **Push to Open**

In order to maintain the modern bath's clean, hardware-free detailing, be sure to choose frameless mirrored cabinets with magnetic latches.

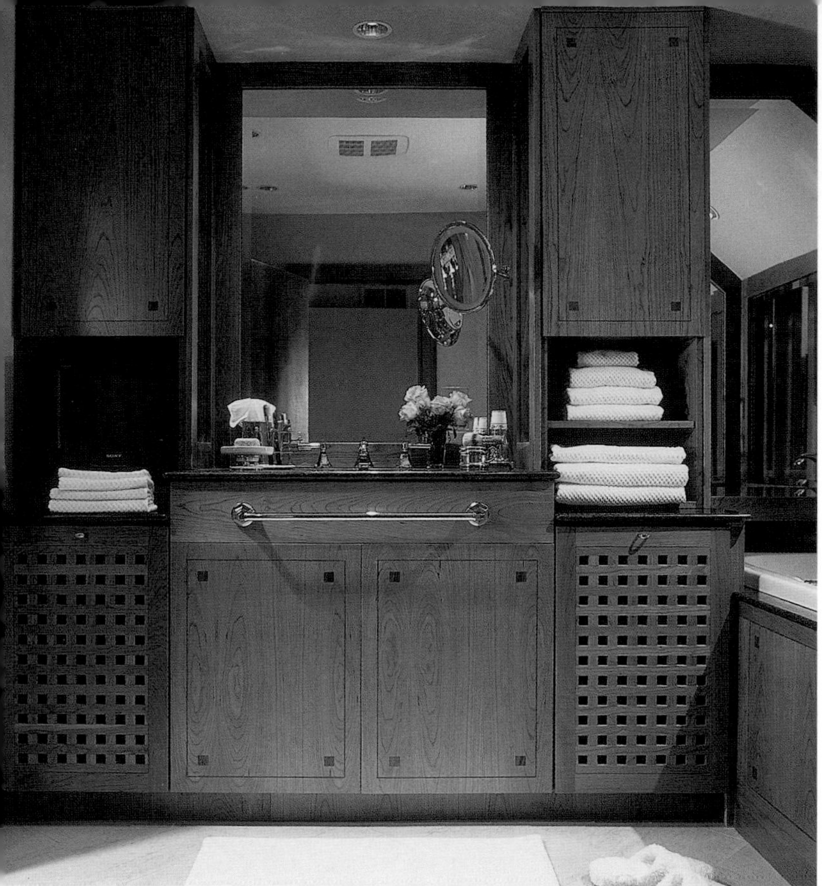

Left: Take advantage of vertical space above, on, or adjacent to the vanity by adding cabinets, shelves, or cubbies.

Below: Include open shelves for displaying attractive items.

A PLAN FOR MASTER BATHS

As the most spacious of all common bath floor plans, the master bath is often dressed up a little bit with a piece or two of furniture that, if smartly selected, can do double duty in the room. At a makeup area, a vanity bench with a hinged upholstered seat can offer a ministorehouse of extra hand towels or tissues. Or tucked into a corner, an étagère can keep stacks of fresh towels ready.

For a master bath with a double vanity, the countertop between the lavs provides space for additional built-in storage. While this option sacrifices some surface space, it may be worth it. One such design is a tall cabinet that can be installed at a right angle to the wall, with doors that open on both sides; alternatively, leave off the doors if they block natural light.

Another design separates the lavs by creating a pillar of storage: stack a 6- to 8-inch-deep cabinet with a door or open shelves on top of several drawer units.

SMARTtip Tissue Niche

Carve out a couple of recessed shelves from a privacy half-wall. They make a convenient spot for an extra roll or two of toilet paper.

FAMILY-FITTING IDEAS

In a bath that's shared by several people, it's a wise idea to allocate storage space to each individual. Labeling drawers and shelves with names is one approach; for young children, assign each of them a colored plastic bin or tub set on an open shelf to act as catchalls for their supplies. Apply the same color-coding strategy to their towels, or use monogrammed linens to encourage organization.

CORRALING DIRTY LAUNDRY

If family members are in the habit of changing clothes in the bath, it's particularly important to install an ample built-in hamper in the room so that no one has to step over and around piles of soiled blue jeans, stinky socks, and sweaty baseball jerseys. One approach is to incorporate one or more tip-out wire bins either in the vanity (although depending on its size, the sink's below-deck plumbing could get in the way) or as part of a bank of floor-to-ceiling cabinetry. This yields a tidy, uncluttered look that can be seamlessly integrated into any style of decoration and avoids the abrupt (and dated) appearance of a freestanding hamper in the bath.

Cabinetry of this kind not an option for you? It's time to think small and separate laundry containers. Hang one or two minibags, which are often

Above: Sleek cabinets suit the contemporary bath. Hardware doubles as a towel bar.

Left: Use open storage to keep nice linens on view. They add a splash of color, here.

printed or embroidered with an attractive motif and can be as charming as they are practical, on a wall that would otherwise be dead space. This combines a decorative touch with storage that is eminently serviceable. On washdays, these nylon or cotton bags can be quickly emptied into a large basket—and the laundry will be sorted already.

BUILT-IN STORAGE

Another built-in storage stretcher is what professional bath designers often refer to as a banjo shelf. This is a physical extension of the vanity counter and, thus, fabricated from the same material: the surface tapers from a full, sink-sized depth down to about 6 to 8 inches—approximately the depth of the toilet tank. In fact, this "neck" of the banjo shelf stretches over the top of the length of the tank. A

All photos this page: With a bit of planning, even odd-shaped nooks and small slivers of space between the wall studs can be coaxed to function as convenient built-in storage niches. Plan for the various shapes and sizes of the items that need accommodation in the bath.

banjo shelf is permanently adhered to the wall. When making plans to include this kind of design feature, leave adequate clearance so that the lid of the toilet tank can be lifted or removed without difficulty when repairs to the flapper are necessary. A banjo configuration is especially useful in small power rooms, half-baths, or rooms where shelf or counter space is at a premium.

TOWELS

No one likes to fumble or stretch across the room for a bath towel as they emerge dripping fresh from the shower or bath. Locate at least one substantial towel bar within an arm's reach of the shower enclosure or tub. Mounted at approximately shoulder height, it will be conveniently positioned for bathers to easily find the towel. Alternatively, a fixture that combines a shelf with a couple of staggered hanging bars can put three times the number of thirsty towels at your service than a single bar. If a shortage of open wall area precludes a full-length rod, use hooks that match the rest of the room's hardware.

SAFETY STORAGE

It's a given that in a family bath, medications must be stored securely. At least one manufacturer offers medicine cabinets that are fitted with keyed metal lock boxes, which can offer some peace of mind when storing drugs or razor blades in a bath that's used by kids. And bathroom cleaning supplies of all kinds must be stored under lock and key or on the highest shelf, away from curious little people.

The Artful Bath

The urge to personalize your living spaces extends to the bathroom. Because it's on occasion used as a place of contemplation and relaxation, it's an appropriate spot to showcase a collection of small artworks or decorative objects. Because it's usually one of the more intimately scaled rooms in the house, with well-defined limits to usable wall space, collections of all kinds take on a heightened visual impact. They should be planned with thoughtfulness and care.

Before discussing the hows of displaying items in a small space such as the bath, take a moment to examine what is and is not appropriate to hang on the walls. No, this is not an aesthetic inquisition; it's certainly not written in any book of rules that a suite of framed Audubon prints is "better" than a series of laconic New Yorker cartoons or scenic views of the back nine at St. Andrews. Rather, use caution in putting original works—such as fine photographs, one-of-a-kind collages, or children's art projects—up on the walls. The reason? Because the bath is transformed into a steamy, moist space on a regular basis, delicate or treasured pieces can be easily blighted by dampness and may result in a fatal case of mildew. The risk of damage is greater if the ventilation in the room is less than ideal. (A vented system is recommended by professionals, but at least install an exhaust fan that is an adequate size for the room.) But don't think that you must forego putting treasures such as these on display altogether; just have a first-rate copy shop make color copies of the pieces. By doing so, you will be able to replace any picture with another photocopy, and still retain the original piece, unharmed.

Plot your bathroom wall displays as you would in any other room of the house: pin kraft-paper templates of each work up on the wall, moving the various pieces around until you are pleased with the composition. Again, because of the bath's tendency towards humid conditions, avoid any frames that have intricate carvings—their crevices and contours will only act as a grime magnet, and your display will suffer accordingly. Opt for classic, inexpensive plastic or acrylic box frames that can be wiped down easily. Or instead of conventional framed works, you can display objects that are damp-resistant by their own nature: decorative ceramic tiles or porcelain plaques, sea shells, or stained-glass panels.

a gallery of...

1

1 Keep frequently used items near the tub or shower.

2 Freestanding furniture pieces or cabinets that give the appearance of furniture provide storage possibilities.

3 Creative use of even tight spaces can improve storage in small bathrooms.

4 Put the space under the sink to use. Baskets keep towels or supplies organized and hide the pumbing, too.

5 Choose furniture pieces made from materials that can stand up to bathroom humidity.

6 Remember: keep open storage areas tidy.

2

3

4

5

6

1

2

3

4

1 Consider purchasing stock or semicustom cabinet suites designed especially for the bath.

2 Convenient small pockets can hang on the back of a door.

3 Custom cabinets can be tailored to all of your needs.

4 Dividers maximize drawer function.

5 Store hairdryers in a caddy, bin, or basket that you can attach to the vanity or closet door.

6 Base cabinets with a recessed toe-kick allow the user to stand comfortably close for grooming tasks.

7 A shower curtain rod with a towel rack saves space.

...smart **ideas**

CHAPTER 8

RELAXING AT HOME

- THE MEDIA ROOM
- THE LIBRARY

You and your significant other have finally carved out the time and staked out prime seats in your home theater for a private screening of Casablanca or the latest must-see DVD release. The kids' bedtime rituals are over: the stories are read, and the little ones are finally off in dreamland, so the house is quiet. Your favorite brand of popcorn is ready to make; the cabernet is ripe; and the lights are low... "Honey, have you seen the remote?"

If the hunt for the remote or, worse yet, the movie you planned to watch is part of the spare time routine at your house, it may be time to hit the rewind button on your media room's organization. It makes no difference whether your personal Paramount is the domain of a serious movie buff or someone more interested in a PG-rated space epic where Baby Einstein and The Wiggles rule, you'll need to plan suitable storage to hold it all.

On other days your idea of leisure bliss may be an hour or two cozied up in a plush armchair or the hammock out back with the latest biography or bestseller. And perhaps your kids are avid readers, too, with a collection that ranges from tiny cardboard picture books for the baby to the latest Harry Potter adventure. If so, you know that much-beloved books have a way of migrating and seemingly multiplying when you're not watching.

SMARTtip Good Viewing

Locating a video screen in a corner of the room (rather than in the middle of a flat wall) guarantees that everyone will have a good view of the picture without getting a stiff neck.

Your surroundings play a role in your ability to relax and be entertained, whatever your pleasure—reading, watching TV, or listening to music. That makes clearing out distracting clutter essential. This chapter will discuss furnishing a room that is designated specifically for movie and TV lovers, as well as audio- and bibliophiles. Plus, you'll find special tips for making space for all of the related accoutrements.

THE MEDIA ROOM

In the media room or home theater, there are two major categories of items to be organized: the equipment, which, while basically boxy, can vary in size; and the media—discs, tapes, and cassettes—items that, due to their often standardized dimensions, can be tucked away tidily without too much trouble.

There are two ways to go in the media room: show off all your hi-tech equipment or house it in a built-in or free-standing cabinet.

BUILT-IN MEDIA STORAGE

Built-in cabinets and shelves are the most sophisticated way of housing elaborate media systems. You can design them to either blend into your decor or become a high-tech focal point. Amplifiers and mixing boards, disc players, recorders, and video-game modules—every component from sub-woofers to turntables—can be nestled into its own tailor-made niche in an arrangement that is based on your viewing and listening habits.

STOCK CABINETS

When it comes to integral storage for media, the options boil down to drawers and cabinets. In most cases, the aesthetic appearance of the installation will play a determining role in this decision: simply put, drawers bring a horizontal element to the design, and cabinets introduce a vertical element. Fitting them into a composition that is both functional and attractive is the objective.

In terms of design, the cabinetry should accommodate components at eye level for easy operation. The topmost and lowest shelves can be reserved for less frequently used items. If you are designing a custom-built unit, be sure to include plenty of drawers to hold your library of discs and tapes.

Opposite: Semi-custom cabinets can do it all in a TV room. Besides housing the TV and related equipment, this cabinetry houses a beverage center.

Above: Owning a front-projection system is a lot like having your own movie theater. Note the projector on the ceiling in this media room. It requires a separate screen that either drops down from the ceiling or remains fixed on a wall.

SMART tip — Media Stats

When you're shopping for storage racks or other types of containment for your audio and video recordings, keep these standard measurements handy:

Audio cassette case	2 3/4" x 4 1/4"
Video cassette case	4 1/8" x 7 1/2"
CD case	5 5/8" x 5"
LP-record sleeve	12 3/8" x 12 3/8"
DVD case	5 3/8" x 7 1/2"

Right: Is it hip wall art or a TV? This thin-profile, wide-screen model is a sleek alternative to the big black box.

Below: Some manufacturers make furniture designed specifically for a home theater.

Drawers. Easiest for children to use, drawers should be shallow and just deep enough for one layer of storage. The idea is to discourage piling up discs and tapes because too many of them can block visual access to the drawer's contents—a fatal blow to any storage situation.

Pullouts. In a home theater, standard-depth cupboards also pose an invitation to overcrowding. Pullout pantry cabinets, which are available in a wide range of heights and widths, can be sized to fit collections to a T. To be sure, it's not practical—or even possible—for everyone to deed over significant amounts of cabinet space for a home theater. If you think your system will change somewhere down the line, hold off on committing to a built-in design unless you anticipate those changes and allow for them in the design.

SAFE SHELVES

When using shelf units or freestanding bookcases to house media components, there are a couple of special considerations to bear in mind. When storing electronics that are both fragile and heavy above waist height, it's vital that the shelving be stable and strong. Many manufacturers provide information on the maximum load a shelf can safely support, so know how much each piece of your equipment

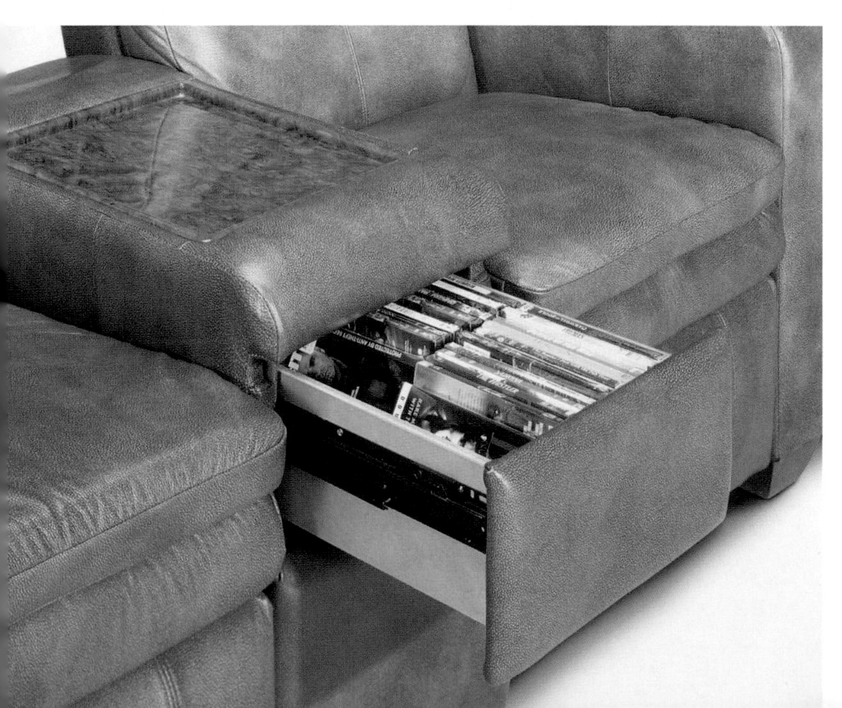

SMART tip **Too Confining**

Avoid disc organizers that have preformed slots because boxed sets won't fit into them. Also, if your collection is alphabetized, you'll have to move every disc to accommodate each new addition.

Above: Freestanding entertainment furniture can accommodate numerous components.

Below: These divided bins roll out to the user for easy retrieval of the contents.

weighs (and bring along component dimensions) when you are shopping for storage. And it's always a good idea to attach a tall bookcase to the wall, so it won't topple over. Now is not the time to cut corners on installation: locate a stud and anchor the bookcase to it.

Regardless of whether you've opted for built-in or standalone storage for your electronic gear, make sure there is adequate ventilation for all the modules. If there's not at least one inch of open space on all sides, they may overheat, which hastens the demise of the circuitry.

CONCEAL THE TV

When not in use, large TV monitors can look like big ugly black boxes. It is possible to hide smaller televisions behind the doors of a TV cabinet. Very large screens should probably be housed behind pocket, tambour, or

Above and right: The doors and pullout drawers completely conceal the media center. When open, they reveal a large format TV and floor-to-ceiling racks for videos and discs.

SMARTtip Room to Grow

If you don't make allowances for expansion of your collection when forecasting your storage space, you could be caught short by the time the next Book of the Month Club selection arrives. Once you've calculated how much space your current media consume, tack on an additional 20 percent for future acquisitions.

concealed doors. Large cabinet doors that swing into the room can obstruct traffic or the view of the TV screen from portions of the room.

Flat-panel TV monitors are only a few inches thick. Their sleek design allows you to enjoy a big-screen theater without sacrificing a lot of floor space.

Above: Plan plenty of seating, and include dimmable lights to ensure comfortable use of the media room.

When disorganization disrupts the intended experience of the home theater, media room, or your library, be it a single shelf or a single room, start to reclaim a sense of order by taking three simple steps.

ONE Sift. Gather all the duplicate recordings and titles and donate them to an organization that can put them to good use. While the major household-goods charities are certainly worthy, try to think beyond them: a local college-radio station might be interested in your golden oldies, or the staff at a seniors' home could be looking to expand their residents' reading or viewing list. This advice can be effectively applied to your electronic equipment, too: at this point in the twenty-first century, you can be reasonably confident that eight-track tapes will not be making a comeback, and it's all right to pull the plug on the Betamax.

THE LIBRARY

A reading room is different from a home theater. While your home library may sometimes share space with another room in the house (a seldom-used guest room, for example), essentially it must be a place of quiet contemplation. That means no distracting mess. Forget the artful piles and pyramids of volumes that often appear in the pages of design magazines—they're mere artifice. The need for well-organized shelves and bookcases proves you're serious about cultivating a literary lair.

TWO Sort. Once your collection has been whittled down, take the opportunity to give some thought about how you want to organize it. There's no hard and fast rule about the best way to do this; just select a system that everyone in the home can use and understand. According to general categories—all jazz, all fiction, all cartoons—is a flexible, broad-based method that has virtually no limitations. The more disciplined and detail-oriented among us can go a little further in their filing; within these topical groupings, items can be ordered alphabetically by author or artist.

THREE Measure. Take stock of the dozens—possibly hundreds—of discs and tapes and volumes that are to be stored. Stack them up, and measure how many linear feet of space will be needed to accommodate all of them. When measuring equipment, don't forget to take into account the wiring run-outs; otherwise, you run the risk of not having enough room between the wall and the electronic unit for the cords and cables.

Above: A wall of custom cabinetry integrates the large-screen TV into this room.

Opposite: Create an instant library by adding freestanding bookcases to the corner of any room.

The Care of Books

Here are some guidelines for keeping your library—whether it's an entire room lined with built-in bookcases or a single shelf unit next to a cozy chair—in good shape. Remember: books are sensitive to many environmental factors.

- Because humidity and extreme temperatures are their enemies, try not to position bookcases against an outside wall, which is often prone to temperature fluctuations.
- Shield them from strong light (natural or artificial) to keep the bindings from fading.
- To prevent warping, stand books of like sizes together on a shelf packed neither too tight nor too loose.
- Don't push books all the way to the back of shelves where ventilation might be minimal; over time, mold could form.
- Fragile or large and heavy volumes should be stored flat.
- For an elegant touch, display a particularly significant or attractive book on an atlas or dictionary stand.

ARTS & IDEAS
COUNTRY

Above: Because space may be at a premium in your home, you could keep some of the books you are currently reading on the extra shelves flanking a TV cabinet.

SET UP A SYSTEM

How you organize your home library can vary as long as the system makes sense to you. But first you'll need to take inventory of all your books to do the job right. Give away all of the books your children have outgrown and that are in good enough shape to pass along to others. Ditto for books about hobbies you are no longer interested in or the novels you've tried to read twice and just couldn't get into enough to keep trying. Console yourself with this thought: you are making room for newcomers. Next, stack those that remain by categories: start with the broadest and narrow down—fiction, nonfiction, biography, poetry—then subdivide by author or topic. If your collection is really large, you might want to file by the Dewey decimal system.

Keep all your general reference books, such as the dictionary, thesaurus, and atlas, together. And group reference books on a single topic, such as nutrition or parenting, on one shelf. Plan a single spot for all your collectible volumes, such as first editions, autographed copies, or childhood favorites.

SMARTtip — Lender's Tip

The heart falls when a gap appears on the bookshelf, signaling that a loaned volume has not been returned. Remember, part of being organized is not losing things. Use bookplates inside your books to remind the borrowers where they got the volume. And keep a written record of who's borrowed what.

Finally, arrange your collection so that the books you use most frequently are stored on the most accessible shelves.

Bookends. On-the-shelf organization can benefit greatly from a surprisingly humble device: the bookend. Available through library supply outlets, color-coded bookends that clamp around the edge of the shelf are inherently flexible and always visible. And look at home goods stores and the larger book chain stores for attractive, functional, and decorative bookends. By contrast, fixed shelf labels can be outdated as your collection expands.

Computer Cataloging. There are several well-respected computer-based cataloging systems that are suitable for the residential library. (Some can be adapted to keep track of music and movies, too.) You can customize them to display the data that's important to you—beyond the basics of title, author, and topic, the collector might want to add a note about a volume's condition, its provenance, and the like. For those who have more books than time to read them, keeping a running list of the read and unread titles in your library can be a helpful exercise.

Avid readers can find computerized "card files" at www.fnprg.com, www.bookorganizer.com, and www.collectorz.com.

DIVIDE AND CONQUER

If you and/or your family members love books but don't have a room to dedicate as a library, include bookcases in several rooms and plan to divide up your holdings and store books where they will be used. Put the books in the room where you are most likely to use them, such as hobbies and travel in the family room or den and cookbooks in the kitchen. Store the kids' books in their rooms for bedtime reading; put books awaiting your attention in the bedroom; and place reference volumes in the home office. Be sure to include some books on a shelf in the guest room. Local lore, history, travel, essays, and short reads could be stored there to keep guests entertained.

SMART tip **Hidden Sound**

The most space-conscious solution for audio speakers is, of course, to recess them into the ceiling or wall. Consult with a professional before attempting to do this yourself, as there may be electrical code issues involved.

a gallery of smart ideas

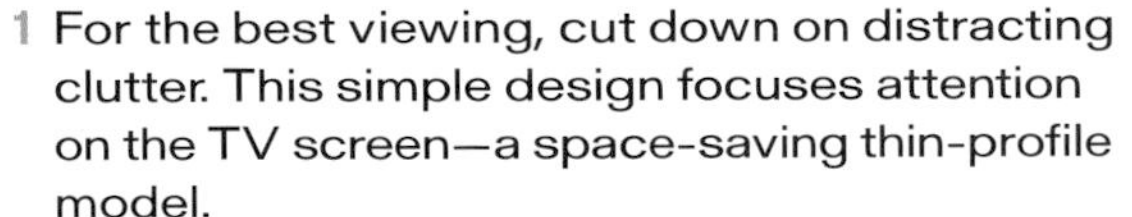

1 For the best viewing, cut down on distracting clutter. This simple design focuses attention on the TV screen—a space-saving thin-profile model.

2 Flat-panel TVs can hang on the wall and occupy little floor space.

3 A larger media room calls for a large television screen. Select a screen suitable for the space available. Too small, and the picture is difficult to view from all areas. Too large, and the TV overwhelms the space.

4 Now you see the television.

5 And now you don't. This room has two distinct personalities: one when the TV is in use and another when it's concealed behind attractive retractable wooden doors.

5

4

CHAPTER 9

THE HOME OFFICE

- WORK-AT-HOME SPACE
- MINI-OFFICES
- FILE FINESSE

Whether it's an entire room or just a section carved out of a corner somewhere in the house, a dedicated home office is a feature much in demand for today's lifestyles. In some cases, a home office is a full-time affair for a home-based business or as command central for the family. Otherwise, it may be an out of the way quiet spot for the dedicated student, volunteer, or part-time worker. No matter, putting it together should include planning, organization, and good storage. Whatever its size or function, a home office requires a few basic features to make it efficient and comfortable—and to keep it that way. It's also a smart idea to choose a location in your home that already has or can be easily retrofitted with sufficient electrical outlets, a phone line, and adequate lighting. Proper climate control and ventilation will be especially important on those days when you put in long hours at work. Include a desk with a sufficient work surface for the kinds of tasks you hope to accomplish. Plan clearly labeled, sturdy storage for office supplies and equipment as well as for important files, ongoing projects, and long-term storage of backup media. If your work calls for storing research materials or for keeping a current library of professional publications or manuals, include proper bookcases. Other items, such as products or samples, might require closed storage in stackable bins, closets, or cabinets to maintain a clutter-free work zone.

WORK-AT-HOME SPACE

This type of office should have an atmosphere that's distinct from that of the rest of the house and conducive to concentration. Of course, the realities of business and family under the same roof sometimes collide. We've all spoken on the phone with colleagues while dogs bark and babies squeal in the background. But when planning a home office, especially if you will be running a business from it, every effort should be made to ensure there's the maximum amount of physical and psychological separation from domestic life.

The most important component in creating physical separation for your office is to choose a space with a door. Particularly if small children will be at home while you are working, a door allows you to close yourself off for conference calls, quiet concentration, and client meetings. And that same door will work wonders at night or on weekends and holidays when you want to preserve family time and be "out of the office."

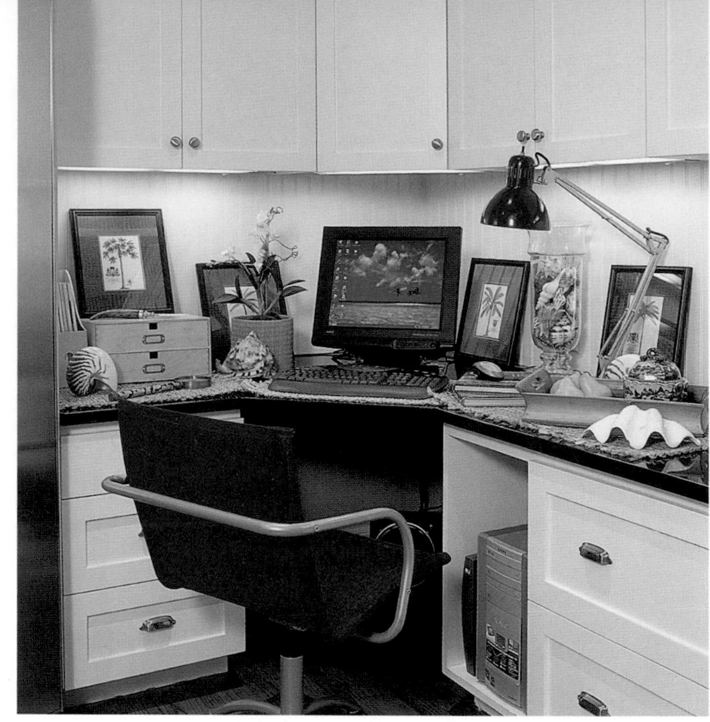

While the right furnishings and equipment are essential for an efficient and productive workspace, there are important related factors to examine, as well. The following Smart Steps may set you on the road to gathering a clearer idea of your needs and honing your organizational choices.

ONE Create a regular schedule. Will you be using your home office on a full- or part-time basis? Are the hours you keep the traditional 9 to 5, an early or late shift, or are they flexible? Will you be working at home on weekends? Integrating your work time with the flow of family life—or around it—requires some thoughtful analysis.

Above: No matter what size, the efficient home office includes both open and closed storage as well as desktop workspace.

Left: If your job demands spending a good deal of the day in your home office, choose the best room in the house. Paint it a favorite color, and add comfortable seating.

SMART tip Maintain Boundaries

It's sort of a home and office shared-space agreement: maintaining a separation between your work and the domestic fabric. Although nobody would expect your desk to disappear completely from view at the end of a business day, it's courteous to acknowledge the resumption of family time, whether it's by pulling a curtain, unfolding a room divider, or closing the door on your workspace.

TWO **Calculate how much space you need.** If you're running a full-fledged business out of your home, you may need space to meet with clients or consultants. Or you might hire an assistant who comes in a couple of afternoons a week. Maybe you work with a partner. Measure the room; draw a floor plan to scale; then select furnishings that will fit the space and accommodate your requirements.

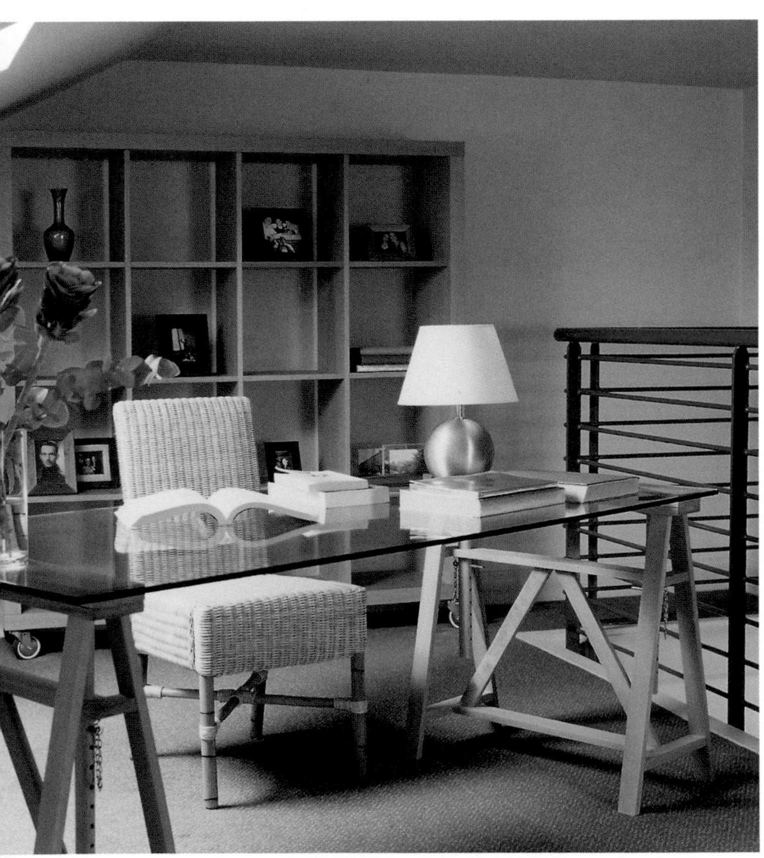

Below left: Even the home office that is used occasionally deserves planned storage to keep it attractive and ready for work when you need it.

Below: The kitchen isn't the only space that can accommodate a family's command-central. Look for a suitable niche in hallways, bedrooms, and other quiet spots.

THREE **Select a sensible location.** More often than not, a dedicated room will satisfy your home-working needs. Which room, exactly, depends on your profession. If you need a quiet environment, an out-of-the-way location such as a finished basement or attic might be the best. If you will see clients, choose a room with an outside entrance or in close proximity to one. Or perhaps a separate building would be even better. (Could the detached garage be converted into a studio or office?) Maybe all that's necessary—or available—in your house is a shared space. (Screen off one wall of the living room, or claim a corner of the bedroom or dining room.) Is a view out the window to the garden a distraction or an inspiration? Will you need access to the kitchen? How about the bathroom?

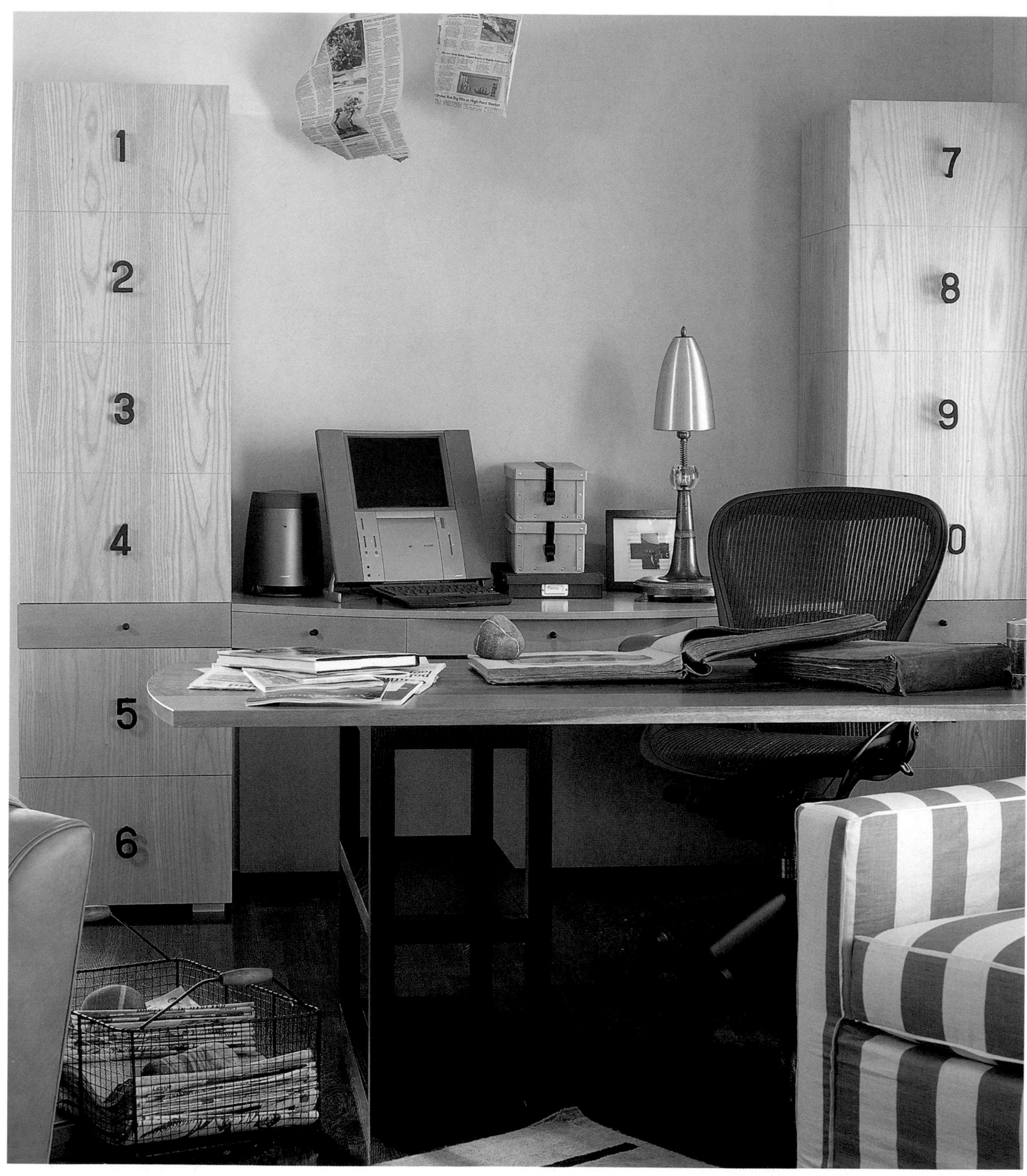
1
2
3
4
5
6
7
8
9

OFFICE EQUIPMENT

Once the big picture of where to locate your at-home office is resolved, it's time to make some decisions about equipment and the day-to-day details of how to outfit your space.

The Desk. The desk is central to any office. Whether it's built-in or a piece of freestanding furniture, a spacious, continuous work surface that allows you to spread out materials is a necessity, no matter what your line of work might be. Do you work with drawings or plans, or is much of your day spent at the computer keyboard? Plan the size of the desktop to meet your needs.

A desk that wraps around a corner or has a boomerang shape puts you smack in the center of activity, a setting that's befitting a Master of the Universe. The next best arrangement pairs two pieces together: a credenza or console that sits parallel to and behind the desk.

The goal is to maximize the surface area you can reach without getting up from your chair. When seated at a desk, most people's reach extends about 30 inches. For both efficiency and convenience, keep your essential work tools and storage for files and ongoing projects within that zone.

Clockwise from left: Whether used to run a business or a home, all efficient offices have several things in common: space to spread out; a comfortable, supportive, and adjustable chair for the person who primarily uses the room; and space for keeping orderly files.

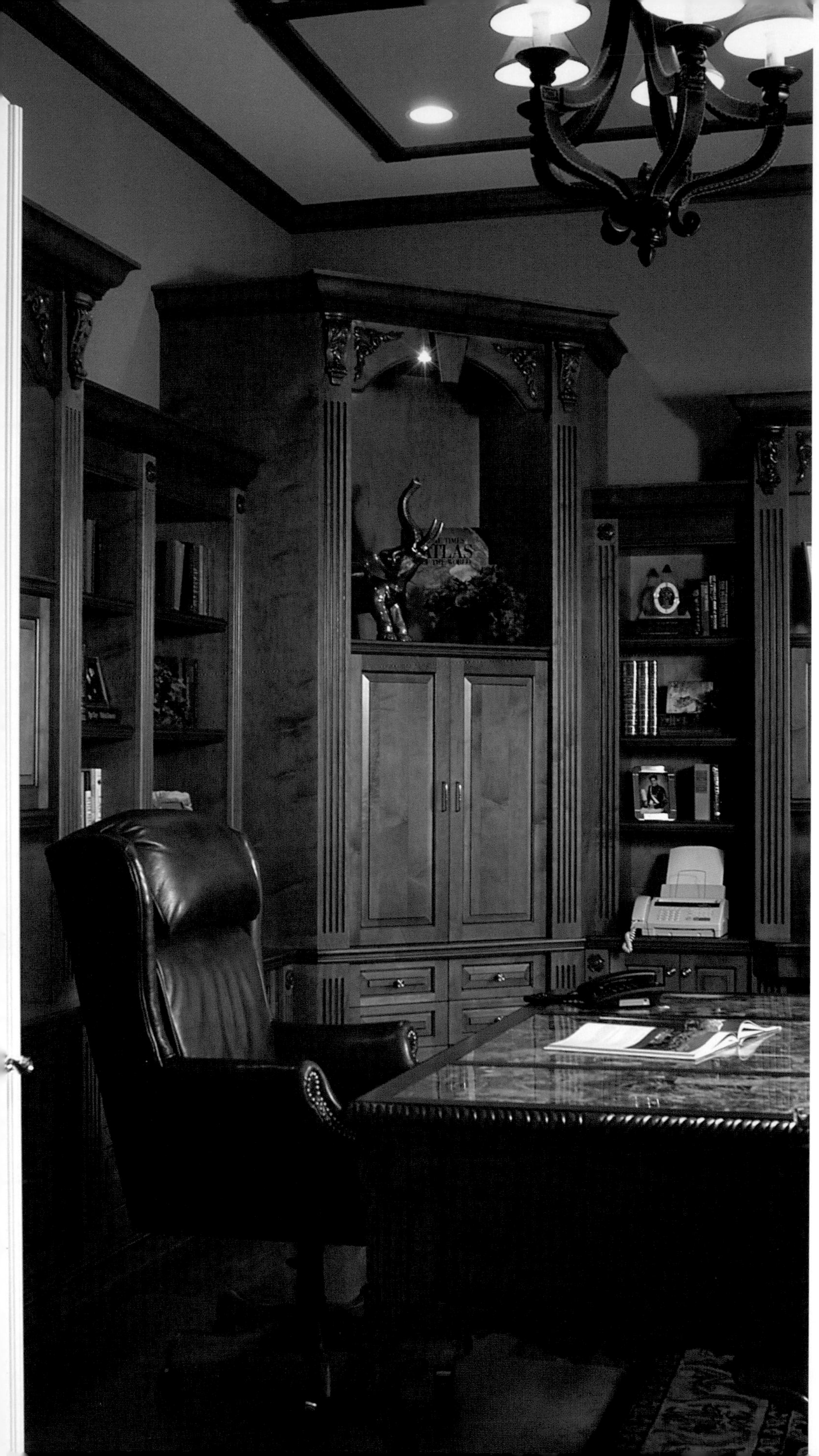

A desk with at least one or two drawers helps corral the necessary small items, such as paper clips, that would otherwise clutter the space. A spot for keeping all the right tools handy is efficient because you won't have to waste time looking for a scissor, stapler, or tape.

Computer Gear Storage. Office and computer equipment should be stored in a well-ventilated, dust-free environment. Because you have to see the control panels when loading or operating the machines, place them at or just below desk height. Using a computer trolley or cart frees up desk space and makes access to the computer's cable connections much less of a strain. Likewise, setting your monitor on a raised, swiveling platform lets you use all of your work-surface area. It's also an ergonomic arrangement because you can easily adjust the position of the monitor to your height to avoid straining your eyes and the muscles in your back and neck.

Wire Management. While the trend is definitely headed in the wireless direction for office electronics, for the time being, cord management is still a home-office concern. Look for desks with built-in chaseways to conceal wires and cables. Desks and work

Left: Custom cabinetry keeps office files and equipment off the desktop. Warm wood tones, good lighting, cherished mementoes, and family photos make time "in the office" more enjoyable.

tables with integral electrical outlets also help to cut down on an unsightly tangle of extension cords.

The Chair. Surprisingly, the most important piece of equipment in your home office is probably not the desk or the computer, but the chair. Especially if you run a business from home, it's likely that you'll spend most of your work time in that chair over the course of a week.

If at all possible, buy a chair in person rather than from a catalog so that you can try it out first. Choose a model with good lumbar support and an armrest low enough to allow you to rest your arms without pulling up your shoulders. If you find it more comfortable, select a chair without armrests.

Choose a seat with some spring to it that fits your dimensions in both width and depth. Be sure you can put your feet firmly on the floor and that the seat is long enough to support your entire thigh. An adjustable seat that moves forward and backward as well as up and down may provide extra comfort. Did you know there are two kinds of casters used on office chairs? One is designed for hard floors, the other for carpeted and resilient surfaces. Protect your floor, and your back, by selecting the right ones.

Above: A laptop computer frees up the work surface in this home office. A wireless remote setup eliminates the hassle of wires, too.

Below: Furniture capable of concealing an entire office in one space-saving piece works well for the part-time home worker.

Office Decor

Storage and style often have a give-and-take relationship. That chic modern worktable you covet lacks a pencil drawer; its clean lines could get cluttered with desktop storage accessories. By the same token, a new flat-screen monitor may look just a little too Jetsonlike on an heirloom Empire desk. But this is your home office, not a corporate cubicle—and happily, anything goes.

MINI-OFFICES

If your home-office needs center primarily around household matters—paying the bills, balancing the checkbook, keeping the family calendar, and so forth—or if you can't spare an entire room, there are clever ways of carving workspace out of other areas around the house.

Look for a location that can accommodate at least the barebones ingredients for a mini-office: a desk, a telephone, an electrical outlet so you can add good task lighting, and a couple of drawers or bins, baskets, or boxes for files and office supplies. Add a laptop computer to the setup, and you're good to go.

The kitchen is the most popular place for setting up a small home office because it's centrally located. Likely locations in the room include at the end of a cabinetry run next to a door, appended to an island, or in a corner deemed too awkward or small for other uses.

OTHER CHOICES, OTHER ROOMS

Beyond the kitchen, there are other potential spots throughout the home for setting up a compact work center. Placing a writing table, lamp, and chair in the cul-de-sac at the end of a hallway turns a remnant, seemingly useless space into a productive retreat.

Refurbish a little-used guest room closet by installing an electrical outlet, a few U-shaped shelves, and a work surface. Tuck file cabinets under the desk surface, and add shelves to the back

Above right: The kitchen often provides the perfect spot for a small desk. Deep file drawers keep clutter to a minimum, and undercabinet fixtures flood the desktop with task light.

Right: Even a small desk can serve as a convenient family message center and a perch for the cook to search for great recipes and compose grocery lists.

The Niceties

Not really necessary, but great for giving your work-at-home space some unique personality:

- Walls painted a favorite color
- Artwork you love
- Framed family photos
- Plants or flowers
- A radio or CD player for musical inspiration
- A coffee maker or electric teakettle
- A yoga mat for stretch breaks
- A window with a view

wall for extra storage. Install double doors with hinges that allow the doors to open fully for easy access. It's an efficient space that can be hidden from sight when it's not in use.

Consult an architect to see whether it is possible to shoehorn a workspace into the cavity underneath the stairway. The ever-adaptable armoire can be fitted with a sliding keyboard tray, mail-sorting cubbies, shelves, and drawers for hanging files. Or search home goods and office-supply catalogs or furniture showrooms for a tall one-piece unit. They're available to suit many decorative styles. These armoires are as efficient as the traditional old rolltop desks—but supersized.

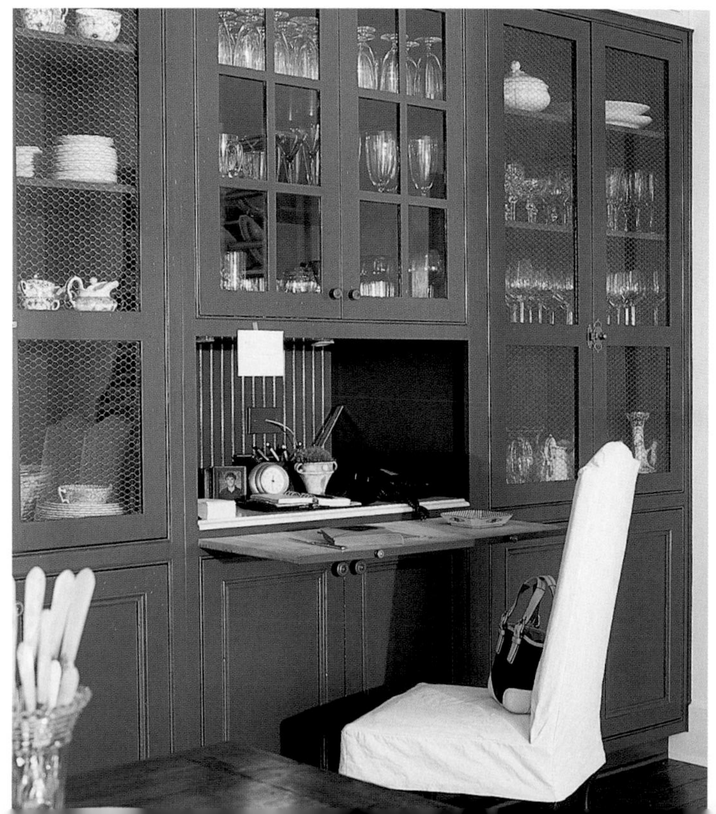

Above: The office's location is limited only by your imagination. Add a desk, cabinets, and electrical outlets to turn a closet into a home office that's hidden behind doors after hours.

Right: Small but still functional, this writing desk is concealed within a wall of traditionally styled dining room cabinetry.

Below left: Choose storage devices that address your particular needs. Then devise a labeling system that makes sense to you.

Below right: Suit the size of the bin to the object. Small cubbies are ideal for providing a home for objects such as pens, coins, and stamps.

Compact Storage. If mini-office users had a motto, it would be "Condense Creatively." In mini-offices, you can—indeed, you must—abbreviate full-scale storage ideas to fit the tighter quarters. For example, instead of filing cabinets, stack labeled and lidded boxes on top of one another or use letter trays or vertical files. And opt for taller vertical bookshelves and desk toppers to make the best use of the wall space too. In work areas without drawers, portable accordion files can be lifesavers. They are available in many sizes, colors, and materials. In a pinch, a three-ring binder can act as a file when filled with plastic pocket-pages. Many home-organizing retailers offer a segmented bin that mounts under a hanging cabinet and pulls down for use.

Short on walls? Pin-up space can be found on the inside of a cupboard door or the wall above the kitchen desk. It's even possible to stretch the work surface by means of a pullout cutting board or a hinged, fold-up counter extension that tucks away when it's not in use.

Above: Even a sliver of space can be turned into a family message center with a phone, pads, and a display board.

Left: Open storage shelves provide easy access to the gear that's used most frequently. Further compartmentalize with plastic see-through bins.

SMARTtip All-in-Ones

Office machines—like a combination fax-scanner-printer—unquestionably save on shelf space. But if one of the functions goes on the fritz, you lose the services of them all while the equipment is being repaired. Consider both the upside and the downside before purchasing major equipment.

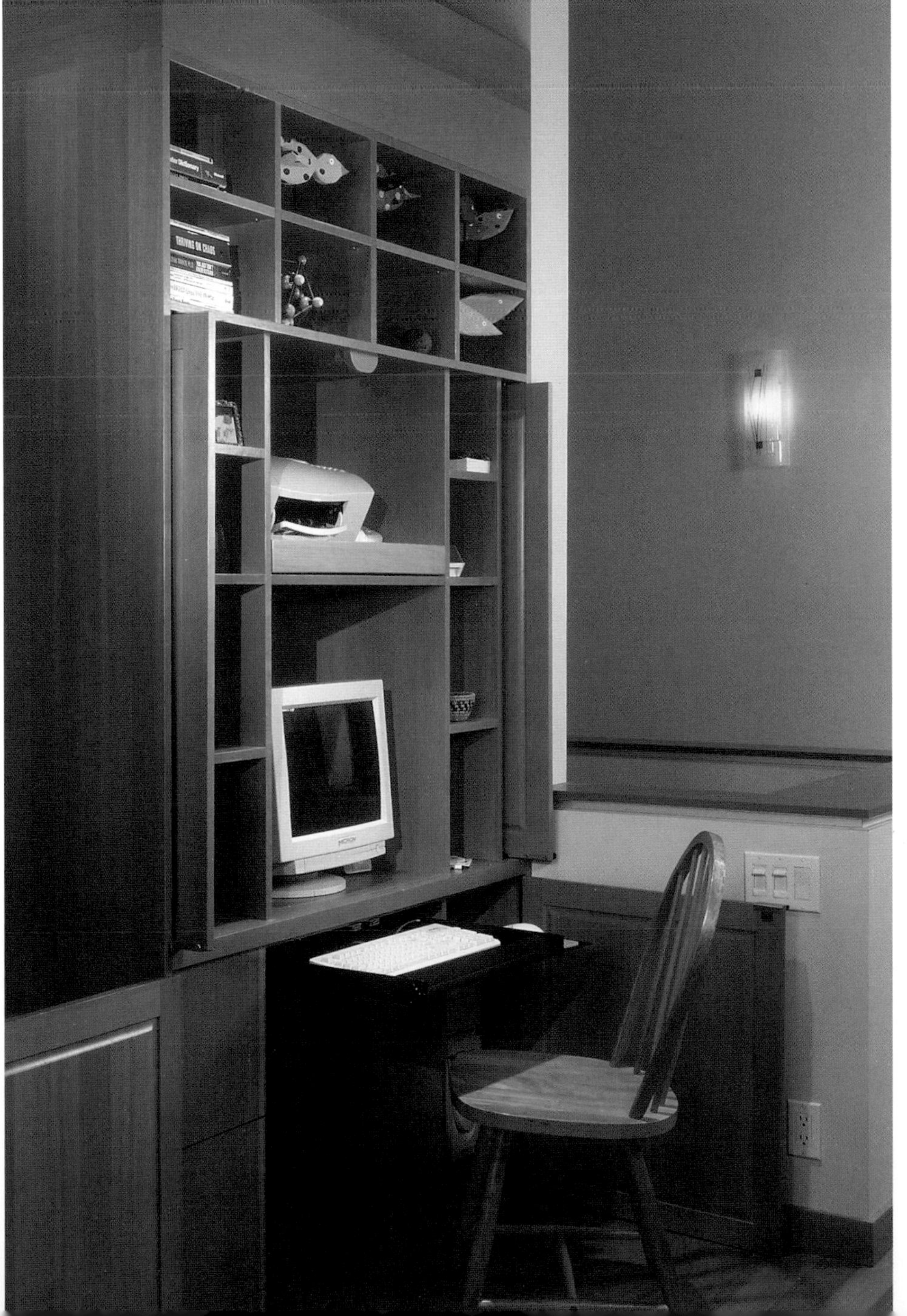

ANTICLUTTER CAMPAIGN

Anyone who works out of a small home office needs to be diligent about how much paper he or she hangs onto and stores there. An effective anticlutter rule: touch a sheet of paper—letter, bill, school notice, and so forth—only once. File it; pass it on; put the date on your calendar; recycle it; do whatever is necessary to dispense with it. And think twice before printing out an e-mail: it creates one more piece of paper to handle. Make every effort to go through mail as it comes. If you are not interested in the promotional materials, deposit them promptly in the recycling bin, ideally located right where the mail is sorted.

Magnetic bulletin boards, cork pin-up boards, wipe-off marker boards: there are a host of helpful devices out there to make the most of the walls in your office, no matter its size or decor.

When it comes to using desk storage space, experts say it's a sound decision to keep your stash of office supplies limited to what you will use in a few weeks. Don't cut it so close to the bone that you have to run out every other day at lunchtime to pick up some items. But on the other hand, hoarding a year's worth of printer cartridges just takes up valuable space that might be put to better use.

Left: Custom cabinets are an efficient way to conceal a computer in any room. Include a keyboard pullout tray and storage cubbies behind pivot-hinged doors.

FILE FINESSE

Remember the promise of the paperless workplace? All we'd have to do to be productive was plug in the computer—that terribly tidy electronic repository of data and information—and all would be wonderful. Of course, the reality of that promise has turned out to be something more complex—and cluttered. For both the family command center and the at-home desk jockey, managing the flood of documents is a constant battle. Scanners, printers, shredders, and copiers continue to spew forth reams, and it falls to you to keep it all orderly.

MAINTAINING GOOD FILES

The filing system is another important tool for a home office. If you don't file, you'll soon end up surrounded with paper clutter. Set files up with a system that makes sense to you. Divide drawers by broad categories, and file by function. One simple organizing tool: color-coded file folders. For a quick and easy point of reference, choose a different color for each category. And label all folders clearly with block-printed letters in a nonsmearing, waterproof ink. File the newest items at the front of the folder, keeping the oldest ones at the back.

File folders are most efficient to use if you hang them in a rack that clearly shows off the label. Files that are stacked quickly become a jumble.

Weed dead files out of the active filing system, and then out of your office, as promptly as possible. Transfer them into cardboard banker's boxes; label and date them; and send them to the great filing cabinet in the sky (the attic, of course). Once a year, review these archives and throw out the boxes that hold papers that no longer have a use.

Right: It's possible to combine both function and style so the home office can work hard but still be a comfortable place where it's easy to spend time. Varied textures, an abundance of natural light, and a view all do their part to make the workday easier to face. Sturdy shelves, filing cabinets, matching boxes and baskets not only look great but work hard too.

SMARTtip Space Divider

Miniblinds make an unusual and flexible space divider. Mounted from the ceiling, they can be raised or lowered as the need for privacy arises. Adjusting the louvers lets light through to your work area, too.

SMARTtip Pinup Board

If you're partitioning your office with a decorative standing screen or room divider, cover the back of the partition in cork or felt and use it as tack space.

You'll need to choose at least one file cabinet. Because each type of filing cabinet offers its own particular advantage, pick what's right for you. Match the cabinet choices up with your needs and the allowances of your space. One caution: if your business would be devastated should the files be destroyed, opt for commercial-grade, fire- and water-proof units. If your office is located in a space that allows it, consider building a window seat that incorporates file drawers.

Rolling Files. Rolling files can be wheeled right up to your desk when you're working and out of sight at the end of the day—a plus if your office is out in the open. However, that convenience may be offset by the fact that they have a considerably smaller capacity than stationary file cabinets.

Lateral or Vertical Files. The choice between lateral and vertical cabinets is often tied to the size and shape of the floor plan of the room. If work surface area is at a premium in your office, it's worth noting that two-drawer files—both vertical and horizontal designs—can stretch that space quite handily. If floor space is tight, you might want to choose a tall file. Just be sure to select one that allows only one drawer at a time to open. This safety feature helps prevent full cabinets from toppling over, especially important if there are children in the home. Better yet, for safety's sake, consider bolting any tall files, armoires, and bookcases directly to the wall.

The Circular File. Despite all of our modern technology and a spate of newly hatched storage solutions, proper use of the humble trash can remains a major tool in keeping your office clutter-free. Conceal the office trash in a base cabinet outfitted with two pullout trash bins, one each for refuse and recycling. This is important if your office is carved from a room used for other functions, such as a guest room or bedroom.

Opposite: Some work-at-home professionals, such as architects, garden designers, engineers, and artists require expansive work surfaces and specialized storage and filing systems.

Above: Office shelving, desks, storage bins and boxes, and other accessories are available at all price points and to suit just about every home decor.

Below: This office niche on a stair landing is visible from the living area. It stays neat and safe underfoot by eliminating clutter. Attractive box containers and a filing rack that's suspended from the side of the desk hold important papers and supplies.

a gallery of...

1 This workstation is integral to the architecture of a large open loft where it also serves as a partition.

2 Depending on your budget, use either custom-made or stock cabinetry to outfit the office with plenty of good-looking hidden storage.

3 Recess a small desk into an odd niche or the space occupied by a little-used closet. If possible, include cabinets to keep supplies handy but out of sight.

4 Consider all unused areas, such as wide hallways or landings, as locations for compact workstations.

5 To ensure efficiency for even the tiniest office, use every bit of space. Here, little compartments above the desk can be used for stationery or to hold receipts.

3

4

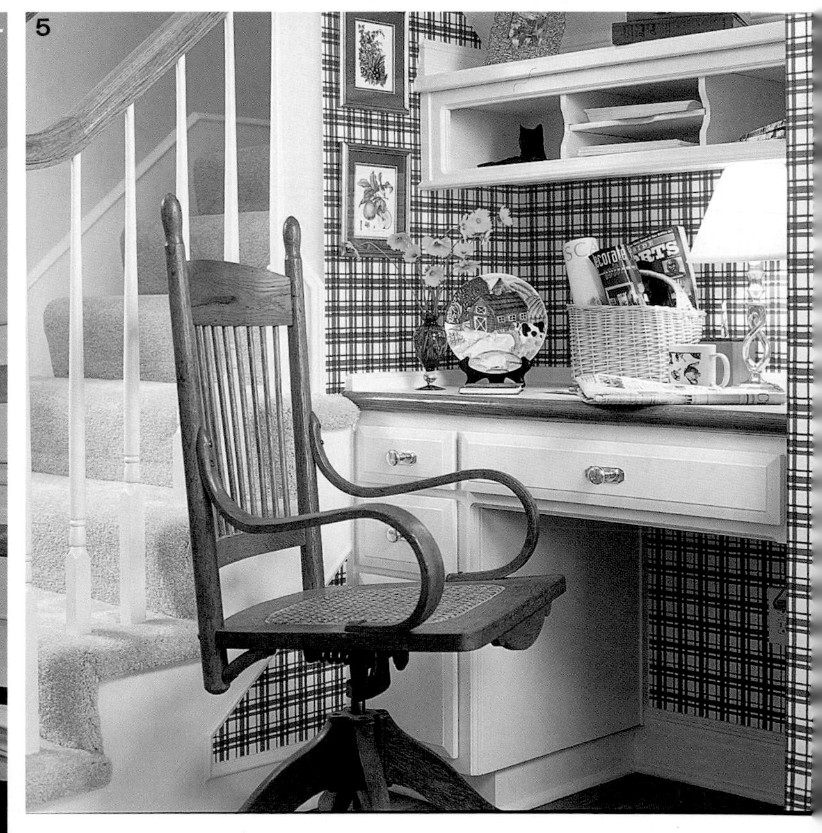

5

...smart ideas

1 A custom-made wall unit can neatly house an office in a living area. Plan tall closed cabinets to conceal unattractive items, such as office equipment and samples, that can intrude upon family time after hours.

2 It's possible to find ready-made office furniture that suits any decor from formal traditional to causal contemporary.

3 Deep baskets suit many decorative styles and provide storage for a look that isn't officelike.

4 Built to your specifications, office furniture can be tailored to your work habits, organizational needs, and storage requirements.

5 Bookcases built under the windows in this airy home office take up a minimum of floor space while providing attractive storage for reference books and a display of family photographs.

1

2

3

4

5

CHAPTER 10

ATTICS, BASEMENTS & LAUNDRIES

■ BASEMENT BASICS ■ ORGANIZING THE SPACE ■ ATTIC STORAGE ■ LAUNDRY AREAS

They are at opposite ends of your home, but the attic, basement, and laundry area have more in common than you might think. Most often they are hidden, hardworking, and overrun with things for which you can't seem to find a spot. The catchalls of so much of our clutter, attics and basements often serve as repositories for our closets' overflow. If not finished for use as family space, both areas are often filled with an incongruous jumble of mementoes, outmoded fashions, and unfinished projects. It's here that you probably stash the out-of-season golf clubs in winter; skis and snowsuits in summer. And where else can you tuck the holiday decorations? In dire cases, basements and attics have an almost sedimentary quality—you can actually trace the last few years of material history by sifting through the stuff stored there. Ditto for those baskets and bins in the laundry area that never seem to be empty of stray pennies, hangers, unmatched socks, and outgrown T-shirts.

Don't let the thought of planning storage for these often-forgotten spaces overwhelm you. With some effort, a few hours of time, and a bit of elbow grease, you can transform these typically haphazard dumping grounds into paragons of storage productivity and organization. Here is what you need to know to get started.

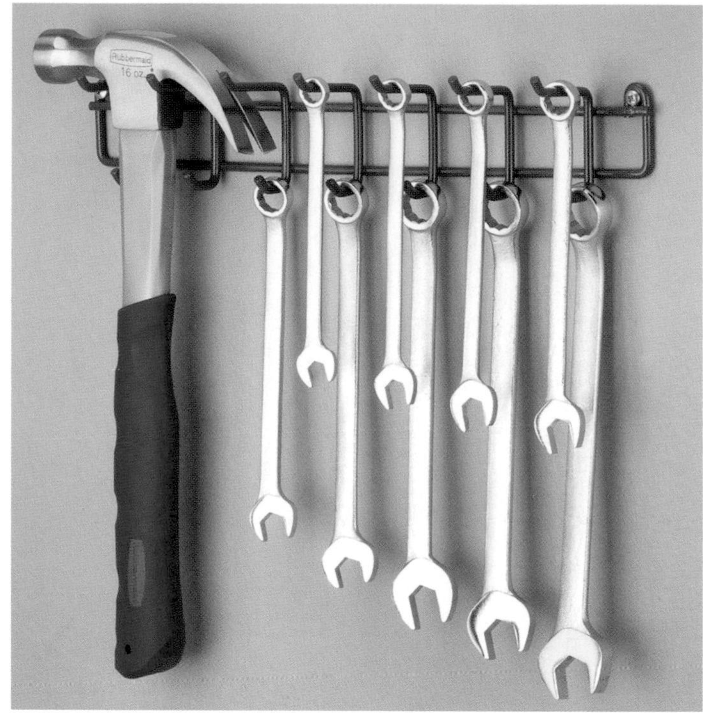

BASEMENT BASICS

Accessible but out of the way, the basement, like the attic, is a prime location for long-term storage. But remember: certain items, such as clothing or paperwork, are vulnerable to extreme temperatures and moisture levels.

UNFINISHED SPACE

Even if your basement is dry, articles bound for that location are likely to be subjected to dankness. As a precaution,

Above left: If the basement is finished—the walls are painted and the floor is sealed and finished—you can probably keep often-used items on open, freestanding shelves. In this basement office, fabric samples and swatches stay neat and at the ready on attractive modular units.

Above: Store the most frequently used items, such as tools, in plain view on the wall in the workshop. This makes it easier for all family members to return things to their proper homes after each use.

Left: A proper filing cabinet is important wherever important papers or records are stored, but especially in the basement where dampness can cause mildew.

invest in a dehumidifier if your cellar tends to be damp. Moisture is an invitation to mold and mildew that can permanently damage clothing, linens, books, files, and any type of film (photographs or videotape, for example). So it's always better to store these items in another location if possible, unless the basement is finished, climate controlled, and contains adequate planned storage for these items.

Clear Plastic Bins and Containers. With tight-fitting lids, plastic receptacles will best resist the dirt and dampness of an unfinished basement, and help keep your belongings from falling victim to the out-of-sight-out-of mind syndrome. And even if you can see through the box, apply a self-sticking label that's large enough so you can list or describe the contents, such as "pool toys" or "picnic gear."

FREESTANDING SHELVES

In the unfinished basement, keep containers off the floor on inexpensive, hard-knock, rust-resistant chrome utility shelves. Looks don't matter here, so focus on function: shop for modular designs—meaning corner components are available—with adjustable shelves.

Raised Platforms. Provide a measure of safety. If you're going to store sizeable items, such as a suite of lawn furniture, put them on raised open platforms to protect them from wet floors, and drape them with a sheet of clear plastic. You can also invest in specially made zip-closure bags for expensive things that you can't replace.

If mechanicals and storage must occupy the same space, keep an open 18-inch perimeter zone around the water heater and furnace. To prevent "detritus drift," put boundary lines of brightly colored tape on the floor around the equipment. Keep at least one multipurpose fire extinguisher handy, especially if you set up a basement workshop.

Above and left: These multipurpose, heavy-duty freestanding shelves and cabinets are made of sturdy resin. They are easy to assemble without tools, and you can combine them any way to suit your storage needs. If you are concerned about stability, you can bolt tall units to the wall.

High-Water Mark

Don't assume that because you have never had water in the basement that it can't happen. Even if your area has never been damp due to ground water, there is always the possibility of pipes springing a leak or breaking, or of a water-heater breakdown or other equipment malfunction that could cause a puddle—or worse. If an item is stored in the basement, it belongs in a waterproof package on a shelf or a skid that's at least a couple of inches off the floor.

Workshops. The basement makes the ideal location for a workshop. An efficient workshop needs good lighting and ventilation as well as organized storage. Many ready-made workbenches incorporate shelves, cabinets, and drawers. Hang perforated pegboard above the work surface to store the most frequently used small tools on hooks and in bins. Keep things organized by outlining the tools with an indelible marker

Above right: A sturdy pegboard and a variety of hooks will hold brushes or tools in the workshop.

Right: There are racks and caddies designed to store all types of tools within your reach on the wall above the workbench.

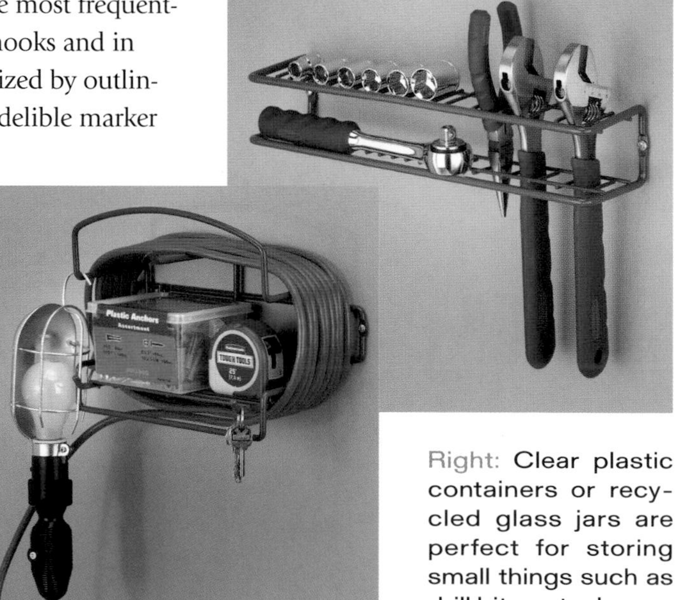

Right: Clear plastic containers or recycled glass jars are perfect for storing small things such as drill bits or tacks.

on the board so that other family members can see at a glance where something borrowed belongs when it is returned. Store items such as screws, nails, and drill bits by size in labeled divided plastic boxes or clear glass jars.

THE FINISHED BASEMENT

Finishing the basement provides the perfect opportunity to create accessible and efficient but still hidden storage. If the finished basement is for living, set aside at least some of the space for an enclosed storeroom lined with metal shelving.

Closets. Finishing the basement provides the option to include floor-to-ceiling closets on one or more walls. Keep them just 12-18 inches deep so items are easy to see and reach. Shallow closets won't intrude on space planned for family activities. For long-term clothing storage, consider using cedar. Before you build, inventory what you plan to store and arrange shelf spacing accordingly. Keep in mind that adjustable shelves allow flexibility as needs change.

Cabinets. Stock cabinets, such as those used in the kitchen, are another option for creating concealed storage in a finished and climate-controlled basement. For the greatest storage flexibility, include both open and closed units as well as tall pieces. Consider optional interior organizers to customize your storage.

Above right and right: **Custom or stock cabinets offer attractive closed storage for finished basements.**

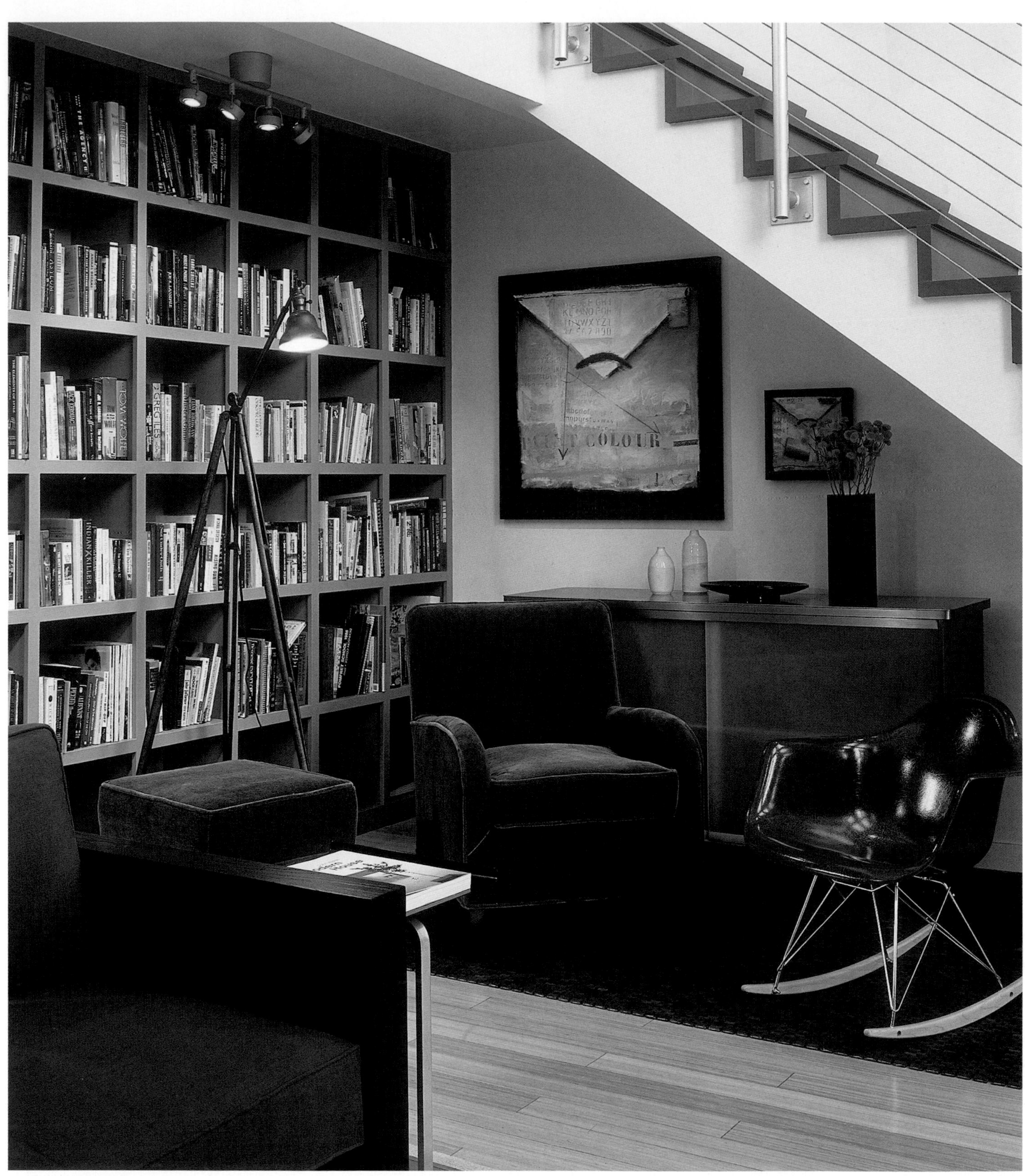
GREG ILES
INDIAN KILLER
COLOUR

ORGANIZING THE SPACE

No matter where you plan to put things, you'll need to get the storage areas in the basement and attic in shape before you do anything. Tackle the areas separately, and be prepared to spend at least one weekend working on each one. Don't move from one to the next until you are finished.

ONE **Do a thorough clean out.** Yes, it's an arduous task, and one that you may have successfully dodged for years. But it's essential if you want to get the most storage out of basements or attics. If you can't face the thought of doing it all at once, set a timer for an hour at a time and clear one shelf, corner, or drawer at each session. Don't move on until you are finished.

TWO **Plan proper disposal.** In some cases, especially if long-expired appliances or left-over hobby or building supplies are being purged, you may benefit by renting a residential-sized dumpster. Be sure to check with your local sanitation department about special regulations involving the disposal of chemicals, computers, appliances, batteries, or thermometers, among other things, that contain environmentally harmful or recyclable materials.

THREE **Divide and conquer.** Decide ahead of time what you will do with the usable items you no longer want. As you are cleaning out the space, organize things into sell, trash, donate, or give-to stacks. If in doubt, throw it out. It might help to enlist the help of an impartial friend on tough-to-call items. Another method for evaluating an object you are considering tossing: decide what is more important to you, the item or the space it occupies.

FOUR **Bring the space up to par.** Use this opportunity to do spot repairs, such as insulating exposed pipes in the basement; fixing a cracked window in the attic; improving the lighting; or adding electrical outlets. Sweeping and scrubbing will deter insects. Discourage rodents by stuffing steel wool into potential entries (better yet, repair torn siding or loose shingles). Now is also the time to consider a fresh coat of paint in a light color to brighten the space even more.

In the end, these improvements will significantly upgrade the storage environment and, indeed, your home. And your belongings will be protected from damage or ruin.

FIVE **Survey the new landscape.** Measure the room, paying particular attention to window locations and changes in ceiling and wall heights. This information will be valuable as you begin to outfit your recovered storage spaces. But before you start bringing shelving units that are already assembled into the attic or basement, note the size of the access or doorway. Openings and entries to these areas may be smaller than those elsewhere in the house.

Left: Control moisture levels and dampness in a basement family room by installing a dehumidifier. This is particularly important if plans call for storing clothing, books, games, and other mildew-susceptible paraphernalia there.

SMARTtip Respect Pipes and Rafters

Don't hang clothing or other objects from the pipes running overhead. And don't compromise the structure of your home by drilling or cutting into exposed rafters to make room for things.

SMARTtip Keep Track

To keep track of long-term storage items, make diagrams of the attic and basement that illustrate their contents and the general location of items within the room: holiday decorations in the southeast quadrant; camping equipment midway on the north wall; and so on, for example. Update the diagrams as necessary. Post the map at the entrance to each space, and keep an extra set of copies in the kitchen or home office for quick on-the-spot reference.

MONOPOLY
Real Estate Trading Game
New England
FIDDLER ON THE ROOF
TAIPAN
ELECTRONIC CHESS GAME

ATTIC STORAGE

Attics are subject to greater thermal extremes than basements, becoming ovens in the summer months and drafty come winter. Because the high heat in an unfinished attic can damage photographs and audio and videocassettes, it's best to look for a spot in the temperature-controlled part of your home for long-term storage of these items. But as a rule, unless the roof springs a leak, attics stay consistently dry, unlike their subterranean counterparts. For that reason, you can feel pretty confident about storing some things up there—yet there are still some precautionary steps to take before you start packing.

PROPER PACKAGING

Wrapped in acid-free tissue and boxed in opaque archival-quality containers to guard against fading, clean clothing will weather storage with little problem, particularly if a fragrant block of cedar is slipped into the package. If in doubt about whether an article of clothing has been worn, wash it or have it dry cleaned—moths are attracted to fabric that has been worn, even if only once.

Labels. Keep track of what's inside boxes with labels. Or snap a digital picture or Polaroid of what's within and secure it to the lid or side of the carton. (This will alleviate

Opposite: In this finished attic bedroom, a long low bookcase is a catchall for books and toys. If there's not enough wall space for dressers in an attic bedroom, substitute with blanket chests, which offer deep storage.

Above: You can make the most of an attic's pitched roof and low ceilings. Here, ready-made bookcases fit snugly under the eaves.

GARDENING MADE EASY
THE GRAPES OF WRATH
MILLER'S
VEGETARIAN
WINE ALBUM
NEW YORK
LONDON
SEASONAL VEGETARIAN
VEGETARIAN COOKING

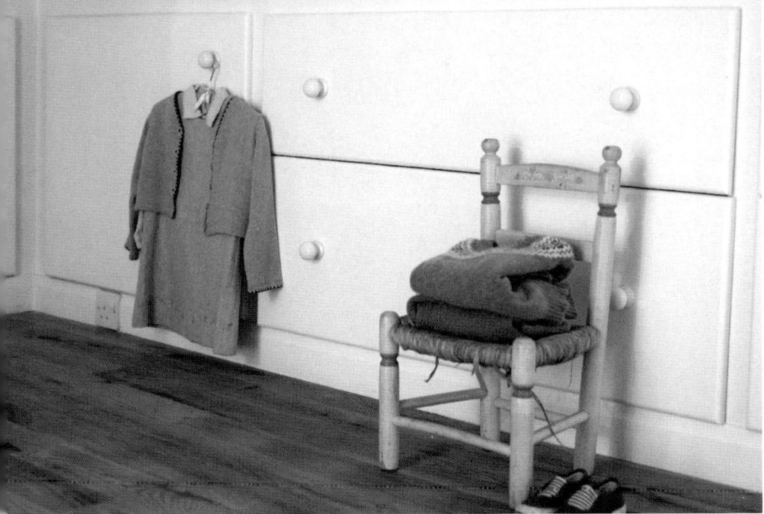

Above: Drawers built into the attic kneewall offer another possibility for storage.

SMARTtip Look Up

Many attics have high or open ceilings that provide a place for extra storage. But only store things here that are lightweight and used infrequently. Items such as empty suitcases, some camping equipment, and cushions from patio furniture are some of the most likely candidates.

any future confusion about just which black dress should be retrieved from storage.) Boxes can be set on shelves or placed into trunks. If you choose the latter, drop a couple of packages of desiccant into them. As a final precaution, just in case the roof does spring a leak, cover the boxes and furniture with a sheet of plastic.

ANGLED SPACES

Up under the roof, space tends to be irregular, with sloped ceilings, dormers, and stairways cutting up both floor and ceiling planes. This can make organizing the contents of the attic more of a challenge. Shelving that can be assembled in a variety of configurations is the solution.

Measure ceiling heights in the low spots before you shop. Select low pieces that can run under windows without blocking the light, and units of graduated heights that can be piled on top of each other against the walls as space allows. Kneewalls present the opportunity to build (or have built) integral drawers that can hold fragile items or things that might be called out of storage several times a year.

SMARTtip No Wire Hangers

When storing clothes, coats, and curtains from season to season, use fabric, plastic, or wooden hangers. Wire hangers will quickly crease the fabrics and may rust or even discolor some of them.

Opposite and above: Use decorated boxes and vintage luggage or trunks to stash stuff openly in corners or nooks.

LAUNDRY AREAS

Increasingly, laundry spaces are occupying a room of their own that's been sensibly integrated into the floor plan of the house. In many cases, it's just off the kitchen; in others, it's set in a converted bedroom, hallway, or closet. Some designers see the new laundry room as a multipurpose space: part clothes-care center; part rec room; part family room. In their vision, this room is used for a range of activities on a daily basis, not just a couple times a week.

That's one emerging ideal. But reality for many households can be somewhat different, with the basement or garage still serving as laundry central. Because these spaces are often pulled in several different storage directions at once, it's particularly important to keep the laundry area—a very active work center where cleanliness is a key concern—well organized and outfitted with sufficient storage.

It's possible to create a functional laundry room even if you don't have an expansive area adjacent to the living areas. Upgrade the laundry area in an unfinished basement by applying some basic storage and organizational guidelines.

Improve lighting by adding inexpensive plug-in fluorescent fixtures to the ceiling. You'll brighten the space even more if you use color-corrected bulbs for the fixture. Consider

SMARTtip High-Tech Help

Technology offers another laundry option, albeit one that's not a full-service wash-and-dry center. Often installed close to your clothing's point of use in master suites or dressing rooms, these are built-in "cleaner closets" that refresh your clothes. Their capacity is limited to a few garments at a time. A system of hangers and special weights excise wrinkles, and a warm, aromatic mist revitalizes fibers. The exterior of the roughly refrigerator-sized appliance can be finished with a mirror or a panel overlay that coordinates with your room's cabinetry.

Left: No place to tuck laundry equipment? Try the bathroom closet. This puts the washer and dryer in close proximity to where much of the laundry is actually generated.

Above: The cabinets in this laundry room store the ironing board and sewing machine when they're not in use.

Below: If you've got the space, a table provides a place to fold laundry neatly. Tall cabinets will let you hang curtains and tablecloths to keep them from wrinkling in storage.

Downy
REFILL
Goddard's
Gentle Wash
Spray

It's the Little Things

- Small laundry aides, such as bleach pens, stain removers, and lint rollers, that are used occasionally can be stored together in a basket or bin.
- Keep a small sewing box with needles and thread in a variety of common colors close by on a shelf in the laundry room so that buttons and snaps can be repaired on the spot.
- Toss all the loose change that accumulates in pockets in an unbreakable bank, which you can keep near the machine.
- Stash all unmatched socks (there's always a few stragglers) into a bin or basket for safekeeping until their mates reappear.

a new coat of paint. Keep colors light, such as gray for the floor and white on the walls. Install sturdy metal shelving to span the unused space over the top of the laundry equipment. Or better yet, buy some inexpensive freestanding metal shelves and locate gear there, where it's accessible to all family members. Another option: install affordable stock thermafoil or laminate cabinets on the wall above the laundry gear and use undercabinet fluorescent fixtures to illuminate the work surface.

Organize Dirty Laundry. Not everything goes in the same pile on the floor. In fact, even filthy, grimy items do not belong on the floor. You'll save time later if you keep various types of dirty laundry separated. Options vary from the simple—several color-coded plastic baskets—to the elaborate—a rolling stainless-steel or epoxy-coated frame with multiple washable canvas bins. Either of these will keep piles organized and out of your way until you get to them.

Left: Improve function by adding some simple wire shelving , hooks, and baskets.

Above right: Stackable front-loading machines can fit into a relatively small amount of space, such as inside a closet, without sacrificing full-size load capacity.

Built-in Appliance Storage. Some appliances offer storage opportunities. Many front-loading washers and dryers are now available perched atop a storage plinth: a deep, often segmented drawer that is convenient for holding detergents, dryer sheets, and other laundry paraphernalia right where they'll be needed. This configuration also elevates the doors of the machines about 18 inches off the floor, which curtails back strain because it places the doors at a height that does not require bending for most people.

SMARTtip Size Them Up

When you are ready to buy new laundry equipment, choose a washer and dryer that match each other in capacity. It makes no sense washing a king-size load if you can't fit all of it in the dryer.

Left: A built-in ironing center, complete with cubbies to stash the iron and related supplies, is the ultimate in laundry room convenience.

SMARTtip Easy Access

Intelligently organizing the essential tools of laundering—the various soaps, sprays, and grime-busters, as well as the iron, ironing board, and clothes steamer—can streamline this chore. A narrow rollout cart that slips between the washer and dryer saves you from having to stretch over the machines to retrieve supplies on a shelf above them.

MAKE MORE SPACE

For laundry areas where floor space is at a premium, stackable appliances can be a boon. A stackable pair allows you to conceal the laundry in an upstairs closet, if conditions allow. Find out if the dryer needs to be vented to the outside of the house before committing to purchasing one of these machines. And be sure to measure any tight turns or stairways that must be negotiated with the new appliance enroute to its new home. If your current laundry set up is a side-by-side arrangement, consider replacing it with stackables to gain space for shelfs with clothes bar below and rolling bins or baskets at the floor level. The appliance switch can turn a small laundry area into an efficient organized space.

Washing and drying are confined to their respective appliances, but what about making room for other related tasks?

Sorting Space. In a pinch, you could sort dirty laundry on the table used for folding the cleaned clothes, but once you've finished one or two loads of wash, a backlog will eventually form, with clean and soiled items competing for the same spot on the table. Balance this equation by either sorting clothes before they get to the laundry room, or with several baskets or bags in the immediate area. Clearly labeling each container according to wash cycles—the basic three: *lights, darks,* and *delicates*—can be supplemented by *brights, dry clean,* or whatever reflects your needs. This will

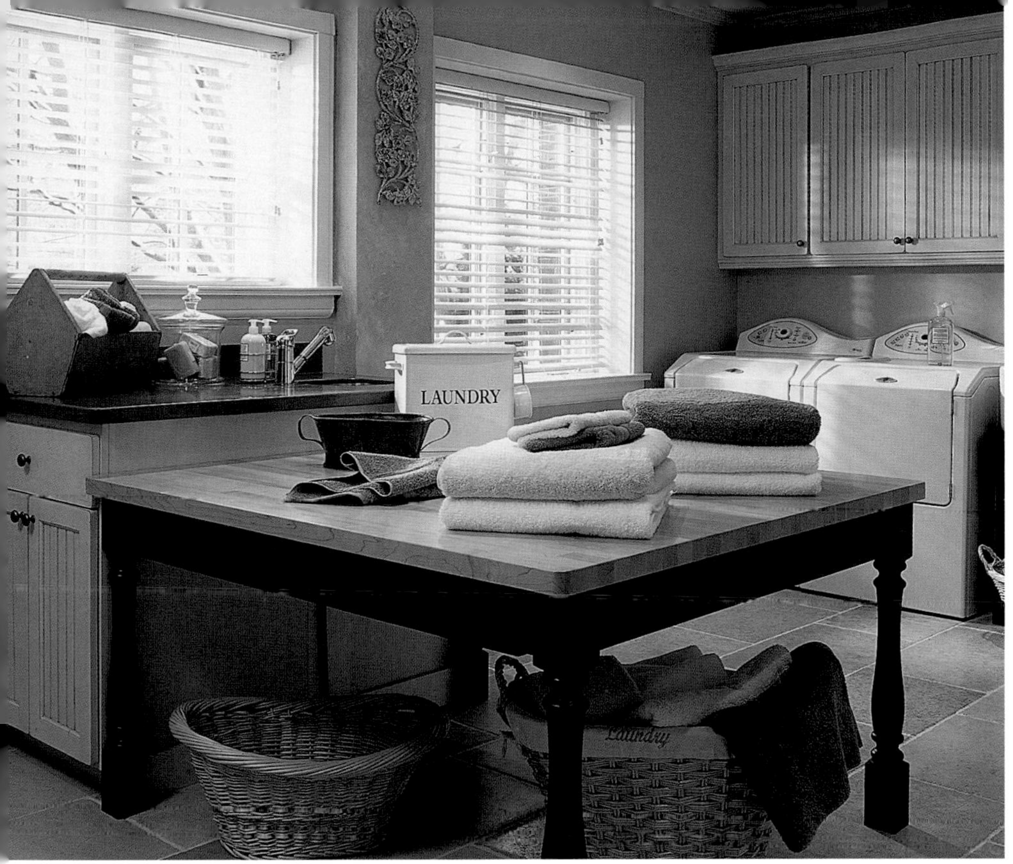

washer: an approach that loses its appeal right around the time when a pile of clean white towels falls onto the floor. If a permanent folding table isn't possible, consider installing a drop-leaf shelf that's as deep as the room will allow to support this function. Alternatively, a rolling cart with a flat surface will do the trick.

Ironing Space. Special racks can store boards and irons on the wall. Smaller, fold-down boards, built into a wall cavity, can be concealed by a door. Another option is a telescoping board that pulls out from behind a drawer front.

help all members of the household to do their part when they toss in their soiled towels and T-shirts.

Be sure to include space for a bag, bin, or basket to store the inevitable forgotten or few leftover soiled pieces until the next laundry day.

Hanging Space. At the bare minimum, the laundry room requires hooks, a clothesline or a rack that will accommodate several hangers for air- or drip-drying items or for keeping just-out-of-the-dryer shirts from creasing. For confined spaces, a fold-down or collapsible wall rack addresses this need. Larger areas can benefit from a rod that spans the space. Or install a retractable clothesline over the sink or counter that stays out of the way when it's not in use.

A concept cribbed from commercial laundromats is a wheeled steel basket that's topped by a hanging rod. When loading or unloading the washer or dryer, this step-saving cart can be moved to the site of the task. Finally, plastic-coated wire shelving provides flat and hanging drying space, too.

Folding Space. Just about anyone who's ever done laundry has resorted to folding and stacking clothes on top of the

Above: A generous table is convenient for sorting soiled laundry and folding clean items.

Below: Install a pole near the dryer so that you can hang up shirts straight out of the dryer. If you do the ironing in the laundry room, reserve a place to hang pressed articles.

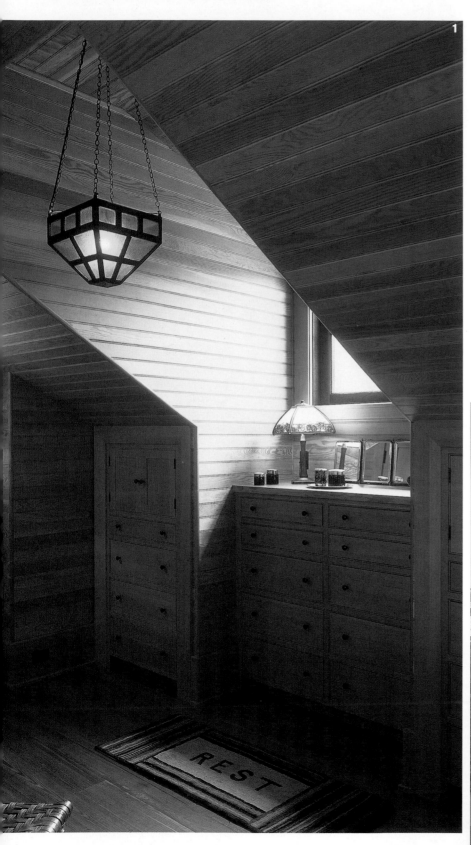

a gallery of smart ideas

1 Odd nooks in the attic are the ideal spot to splurge on built-ins.

2 The back entry hallway is a traditional location for the laundry. It's out of the main work-flow area, but still close to family action centers.

3 Turn a small niche into display space that can double as open storage space. Paint the back wall a contrasting color for added punch.

4 Tuck a study nook under the eaves. Install doors to provide access to crawl-space storage.

5 Modular stacking units offer an affordable storage option for any space.

6 Provide each family member with a coat cubby near the basement or garage entry.

3

4

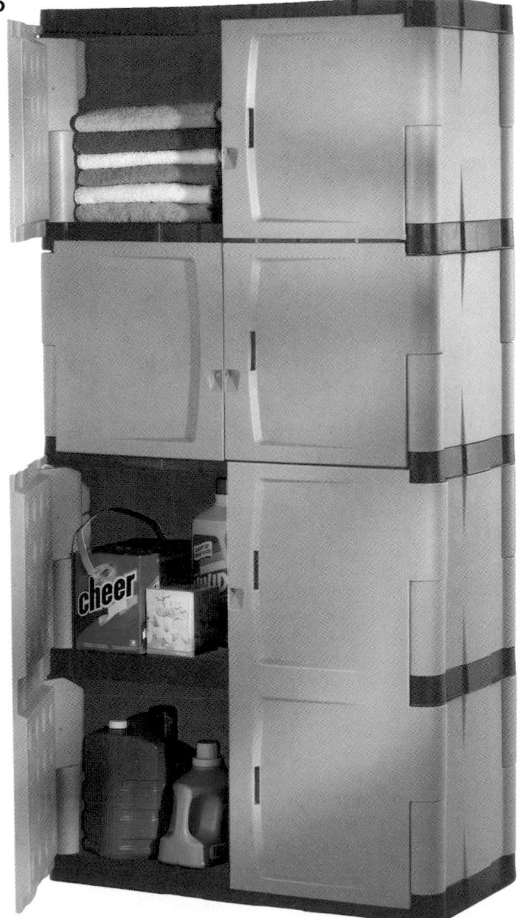

5

6

NORTH SHORE
SXR 740
California
3NSX347

CHAPTER 11

GARAGES, SHOPS & CRAFTS AREAS

■ ORDER IN THE GARAGE ■ RETOOLED WORKSHOPS ■ TIDY CRAFTS STUDIOS

Originally intended as housing for an automobile, the garage has always been a repository for all kinds of accumulated stuff. Now it has morphed into something of a storage warehouse for modern families who have almost turned acquiring and hoarding into a national pastime. In fact, the garage has become so important to modern lifestyles that realtors will tell you that a three-car garage is a big selling point—because at least one bay can be dedicated entirely to storage.

When deciding what to store in your garage, keep in mind that the space is typically uninsulated and, therefore, not climate-controlled. That makes the garage susceptible to dirt, dampness, and a motley assortment of rodent and insect visitors. All of which means that the garage is not the place for off-season wardrobes or family documents, even for a short time. As a rule, the garage is a fine depository for sporting equipment and any other durable, bulky items that see infrequent or part-time use.

Workshops and crafts areas are something else. The tools and materials that pile up in these two similar spaces are smaller, more numerous, and more frequently needed. They require safekeeping and containment, but they have to be handy, too. In this chapter, you'll find storage and organization suggestions that make sense specifically for the garage, and more ideas for the areas where you putter with your hands.

ORDER IN THE GARAGE

Look to the garage structure itself to offer plenty of opportunities to create useful storage. Overhead, open rafters can hold light and large articles, such as odd lengths of lumber, outdoor holiday decorations, rolls of wire fencing, and extra window screens. It's okay to slide a couple sheets of plywood or masonite across the beams to make a more receptive platform. But resist any temptation to stow snow tires or other heavy objects overhead.

For flat-roofed garages that don't have an open ceiling, build or buy U-shaped supports that you can suspend in the areas of the garage where there's sufficient headroom.

BETWEEN THE STUDS

The exposed wall studs offer a forthright framework for on-the-spot built-in storage, too. Short, shallow braces can be fitted between them, yielding virtually unlimited shelf space. Another option: use the stud bay to stash tall objects—snow shovels and rakes—upright and orderly by attaching stretchy bungee cords at regular intervals across the recesses separating the studs.

SMARTtip Secure Chemical Storage

For securely storing spray paints, yard chemicals, and solvents, it's not a bad idea to have a lockable cabinet in the garage. Fabricated of noncombustible powder-coated metal, it will stand up to the uncontrolled climate conditions in the garage without warping or rusting.

HOOKS

Hooks are indispensable in the garage. They'll keep everything from folded lawn chairs to coiled hoses off the floor and out of the way. To avoid damaging scratch-prone items, such as bikes, use vinyl-coated hardware. (If you don't want to lift a bike over your head, consider investing in a pulley system, which makes it much easier.)

READY-MADE GARAGE SYSTEMS

The number of ready-made products designed specifically for garage storage has exploded. Pouch systems are an interesting addition to this array. They function like tool belts for your garage walls. Made of heavy-duty fabric or mesh, they attach to the wall using grommets in the upper corners of the pockets. The appeal of this kind of storage is its flexibility. You can hang the pockets close to your workspace, and then move them once the project has been completed. Similarly, if you've stashed small gardening tools in one pouch, it's easy to grab and carry outside to the azalea bushes at pruning time.

Left: Organize by function, and use a variety of hooks, bins, and racks. Set aside specific storage areas by tasks, such as gardening tools, home maintenance equipment, and toys and sports gear.

Flexible, Modular Units. For those who want to make the garage the quintessence of organization, full-blown wall and rack treatments made of weather-resistant polyvinyl or powder-coated steel can hold brackets, shelves, buckets, hooks, or even cabinets. Taking their cue from the displays utilized in retail establishments, these systems consist of wall panels with molded horizontal ridges that conceal the studs and give the garage a finished appearance. Bracketed shelves and racks fit easily into the grooves formed by the ridges, and they can be moved or repositioned as your needs change. Garage systems can cost a few hundred or many thousands of dollars (for a custom design), so be precise about measuring the space and estimating your needs.

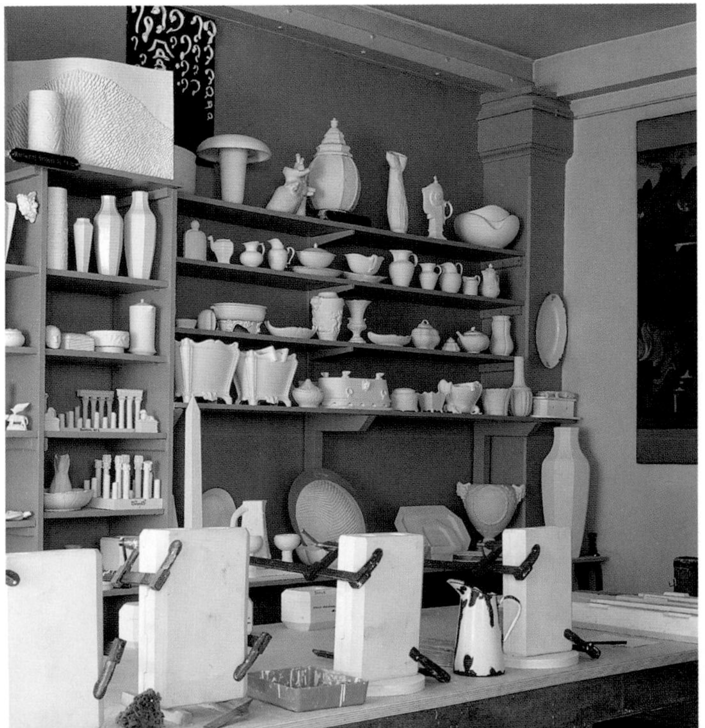

Before mounting your organizational assault, there are some preliminary procedures you should take that will make the process easier.

ONE **Clean out.** Make sure you have plenty of garbage bags and cardboard boxes on hand before beginning the dirty work. To be on the safe side, use contractor-grade plastic bags for hauling away heavy-duty rubbish. Available at home centers, they are larger and infinitely stronger than the type commonly found at the supermarket, and will resist punctures and leaks more effectively. You'll need to have a number of medium-sized boxes for sorting things that don't belong in the garage or wherever you are creating a shop or workroom. Designate separate boxes for items that you want to donate; throw away; sell at a yard sale, in a consignment shop, or online; and relocate to a more appropriate location somewhere else.

TWO **Take measurements.** Make a scale drawing of the space. If it's the garage, measure *with the car parked inside and its doors ajar* so you can determine if there's room to walk. Make similar allowances for any other more or less permanent fixtures in the space, such as worktables, cabinets, lawn mowers, garbage cans, or bikes.

Above: Components of status-symbol garage systems may include trash compactors and refrigerator-freezers.

Left: Many workshops, studios, and crafts rooms require basic, but thoughtful storage. These shallow shelves were planned for a ceramics studio.

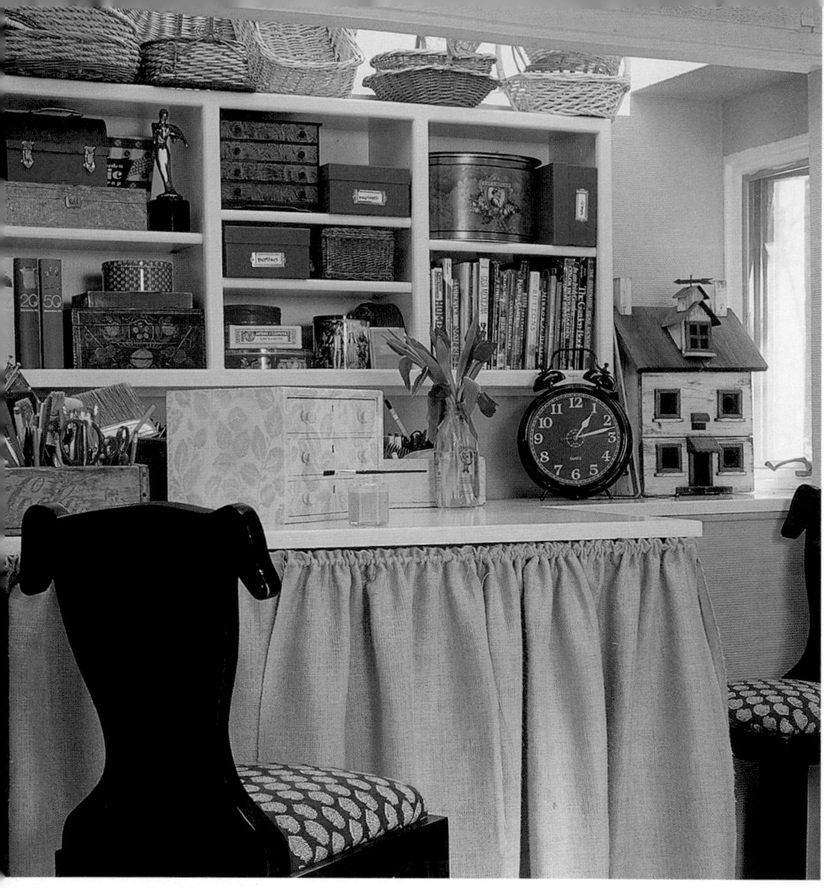

RETOOLED WORKSHOPS

To the accomplished carpenter, the term "workshop" conjures a tidy battery of lathes, miter saws, hand planes, and belt sanders. The word has a distinctively different meaning for an automotive enthusiast, who might envision an array of pneumatic tools, grinders, and grease buckets worthy of a NASCAR pit. While at first thought the pursuits of the carpenter may seem very different from those of the person who gets a thrill tinkering with engines and timing belts, in terms of shape and size, many of the tools and necessary equipment are similar. In fact, the same is true about some of the things that can be found in a crafts studio. (See "Tidy Crafts Studios," on the next page.)

ORGANIZING THE WORKSHOP

In the general-purpose home workshop, typical tasks might range from refinishing a small piece of furniture to painting a child's wagon or rewiring an old lamp. So the need for storing specialized equipment, like the type that might be used by a serious hobbyist or professional is far less. It may simply require some reorganization.

The Workbench. The keystone of any home shop is the workbench. The principle work surface in the room, it's the site of countless clamping, pounding, and cutting operations—and therefore must be kept as clear of clutter as possible. Having a low backwall on the bench fitted with adjustable racks lets you keep the tools and hardware needed for the job at hand, with the rest well out of the way.

Tool Chest. Chests will keep hand tools organized and clean—which, given the common and destructive rust-inducing elements that typically exist in a shop, is vital. Heavy-duty tool chests are available in a multitude of configurations and sizes, from four-drawer stacking units to 13-drawer wheeled carts. Inside, organize your tools by type: screwdrivers all together, the same with wrenches, hammers, chisels, files, pliers, and grips.

Drawers. Shallow drawers of graduated sizes limit tools to a single layer, keeping all of them visible, all of the time. Put lengths of slightly tacky rubber shelf liner inside the drawers to prevent the tools from rattling back into the depths of the drawer every time it's opened. Look for ones with full-extension ball-bearing slides—and give them a few strong test slams before committing to purchasing one.

Labeled Containers. Fasteners, washers, nails, springs—all little, metal, and plastic things—abound in the workshop. Keep them in view, within reach, and off the work surface by stashing them in labeled containers on labeled shelves. Group like items together in miniature open bins or, if your klutzy gene is dominant, in lidded jars or boxes. Now is not the time to generalize: labeling a coffee can "nails" and throwing in a 6d galvanized nail with 3d finishing nails isn't going to save you a trip to the hardware store. Making the up-front effort to sort will.

Rolling Cart. For the workshop that's spatially challenged, mobile project centers pose a possible solution. These rolling units combine the surface area of a workbench with the enclosed storage of a tool chest. More sophisticated designs incorporate electrical outlets, auxiliary flip-up shelves, and, of course, that modern-life must-have: the drink holder.

All photographs: An efficient work studio has a large work surface (opposite). Concealed storage is important if the work and living space is shared (below). Custom cabinets boost organization in a crafts room (right). An indoor potting area needs wipeable, non-porous materials to stay clean (below right).

TIDY CRAFTS STUDIOS

Once upon a time, it was called the sewing room. Now, with the resurgence of so many domestic crafts, dedicated hobby spaces are turning up in a lot of homes. Like workshops, the storage requisites for painting, papermaking, assembling photo albums, and needlework are diverse when it comes to the details. However, once again there are some basic storage precepts that bridge the gaps between different pursuits.

CREATING NEATNESS

Of course, some of the same storage strategies can be applied to both shops and craft studios. Dowel rods or lengths of PVC piping can hold anything that comes in a roll form, whether it's wrapping paper or landscape netting; small, clear lidded boxes or jars are perfect containers for sequins as well as wing nuts; and shallow drawers are equally effective holding sheets of delicate rice paper or a 45-piece set of socket wrenches. Here are some items you can use to eliminate crafting clutter.

Taboret. The crafter's equivalent to the tool chest, a traditional artist's taboret, with its five levels of storage, is essential. Caddies for scissors, pens and pencils, brushes, and more coexist with compartments and trays that swivel out when needed. Casters let you position the compact piece where it's most convenient.

Crafts Armoire. Convert a standard armoire into a customized cabinet that integrates into your home's decor. Once you've taken the measure of all your art supplies, lay out a series of shelves, slots, and rods that will accommodate the materials. Line one of the doors with corkboard or Homasote panel to make a pin-up display.

Portable Cart. Scrapbooking and quilting are often done outside the home at themed parties and social gatherings. Wheeled carts and portable crafts totes convey loads of materials in an organized fashion, thanks to a plethora of pockets and compartments. They work well in the home that lacks a dedicated crafts room, as well; just roll them out of the closet and set up in any room for work.

a gallery of...

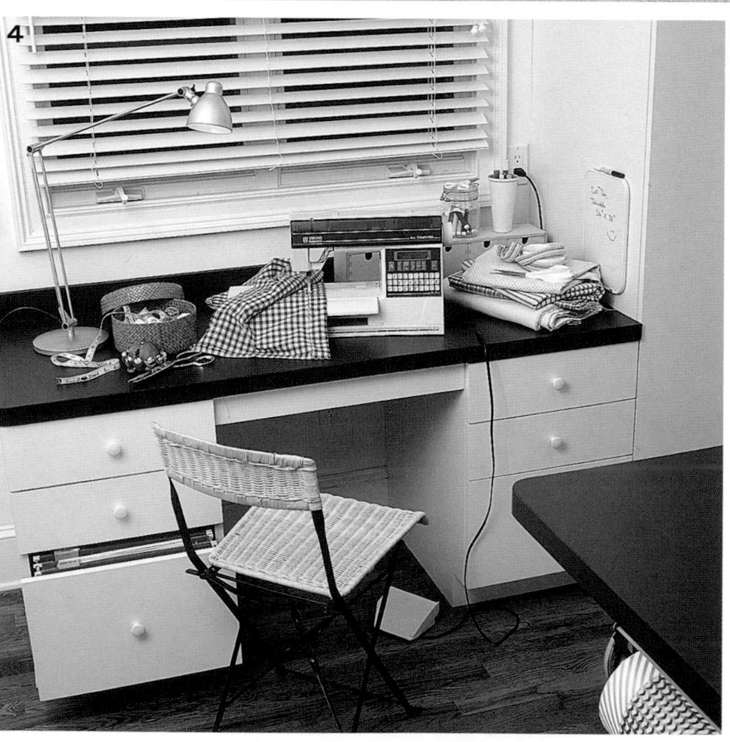

1 A gift-wrapping center can include storage for all of the necessary supplies and a spot to stash gifts, too.

2 Keep the largest, heaviest, and most frequently used items closest to the floor.

3 In a crafts room, cabinets with glass doors keep supplies visible but still protected.

4 Even a compact sewing center can include storage for all the necessary gear.

5 A basic pegboard and hooks provides flexible storage that can be changed as needed.

6 Choose attractive storage components, such as boxes and baskets that suit the size and shape of the materials you need to store.

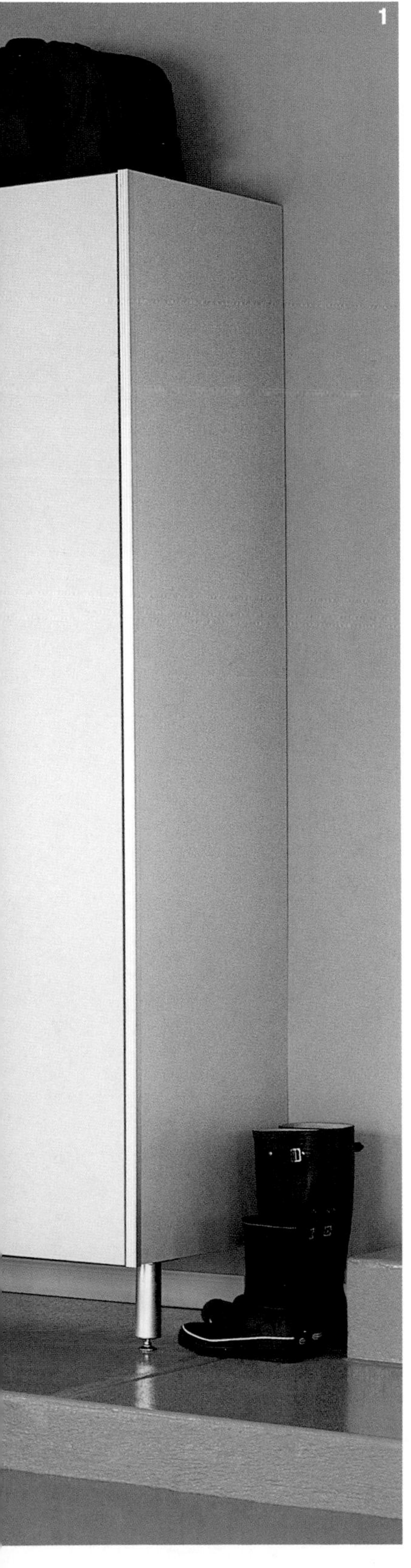

...smart ideas

1 Finished walls and floors can turn a garage into a clean storage space and a pleasant workroom. Locked cabinets provide safekeeping for potentially hazardous household chemicals.

2 A flexible garage system lets you organize space to suit your lifestyle and needs. Tucked into a corner, it serves as a garden center here.

3 Wall racks keep sports equipment off the floor but within reach. Accessories, such as baskets, shelves, and hooks, let you customize racks to fit various-size items.

CHAPTER 12

OUTDOOR SPACES

- SHED STORAGE
- SMALLER STORAGE NEEDS

Whether it's picnic leavings scattered on the beach or an overturned trash bin in a public park, litter ruins the natural beauty of any landscape. Your bucolic backyard vista can be similarly spoiled if it's riddled with a hodgepodge of sporting gear, gardening equipment, trash cans, and barbecue tools.

Whatever its size, that patch of earth behind your home is potential outdoor living space. Planned correctly, even a postage-stamp-sized backyard can function as an outdoor family room. And you'll squeeze more function and enjoyment out of it if you plan storage for the kinds of activities your family enjoys.

It's okay (in fact, it's essential) to adopt a "not in my backyard" stance regarding containing the mess on your property. Even if you don't spend much time outdoors and the backyard remains strictly a play space for the kids, it's just plain good-neighbor policy to contain the clutter and maintain the view from everyone's windows. So don't wait until your neighbors look askance at the growing outdoor disorder before you take action. Apply the same storage principles used inside your home to the outdoors to create a serene, clutter-free personal paradise.

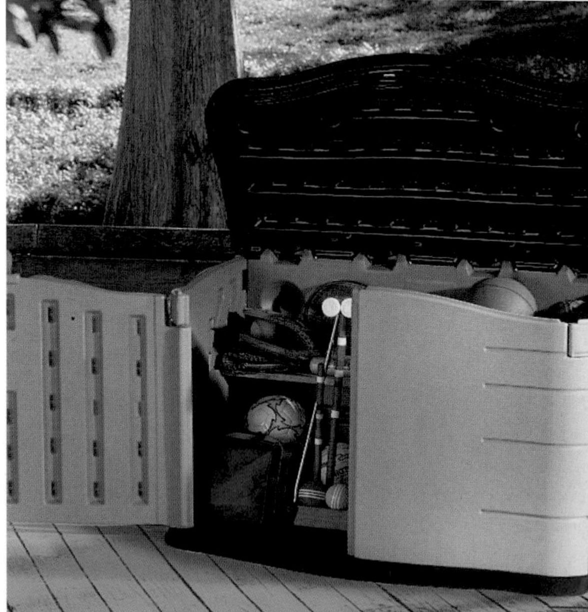

SHED STORAGE

Erecting a storage shed on your property is a lot like building an addition to your home with regards to making aesthetic decisions and complying with local building codes. Many communities have statutes that stipulate where a shed can and can't be located, how large and tall the building can be, and sometimes acceptable appearance guidelines.

DURABLE MATERIALS

Select shed material that is both durable and attractive. Rot-resistant wood, such as cedar, will need periodic maintenance over the years, but it has a strong traditional appeal. If you choose vinyl siding, it should be of premium quality to minimize the risk of warping and discoloration. Steel tends to rust, so use aluminum instead. Keep in mind that no matter how sturdy a shed you select, it will not provide protection from weather extremes. If your backyard is hot and humid in the summer, the shed will be hot and humid inside. For that reason, do not store any valuable or perishable items there.

Above: Tool sheds come in all shapes and sizes to handle many functions.

Below right: Keep aesthetics in mind: choose a style that suits the architecture of your home and/or garden.

Solutions will differ according to the architectural features of your home, the size of your lot, and, of course, the amount of stuff that needs stowing. From a simple deck bench with a lid that opens to store pads and pillows for patio furniture to a freestanding storehouse that's been custom-made into a dream potting shed, there are lots of ways to keep your exterior accessories orderly and accessible.

SMARTtip — Hose Help

House the ubiquitous garden hose according to the way it's used in your yard. If the hose doesn't have to stretch far from the spigot to do its job, coil it into a decorative terra cotta pot or a weathered wooden barrel. If your hose is extralong, loop it on a wheeled cart that can be pulled around the yard as needed, a convenient gardening accessory.

Smart Tip — Garden Tools

Clean garden hand tools before storing them for the winter. Immerse the tool a few times in a bucket of sand, or wash the tool with running water and dry it completely before putting it away. To prevent rust, apply a light coating of oil (even olive oil will do) using a clean rag or paper towel.

CONSIDERING THE SITE

Even if it comes in a common kit form, your shed is a permanent structure that should be as carefully and properly constructed as any other building on your property. The floor slab or foundation must be level; the framing must be square, plumb, and structurally sound; and the ground around the shed must drain properly. If you're not confident in your DIY abilities in these areas, don't hesitate to call in a professional to do the job.

SIZING IT UP

When shopping for a shed, bear in mind the width of the door opening. Does it allow ample clearance—side-to-side as well as overhead—for the largest items you plan to store inside the building?

Plan shelf spacing to accommodate the size of any storage bins. Organize enough space so that you can avoid stacking the bins, making them more difficult to access.

PICKING A STYLE

You can indulge your inner architect when selecting color and detailing for a shed. If it will lead a double life as a playhouse, choose an exuberant design that pairs ornate gingerbread trim with a sherbet-color palette. Evoke a nautical feel appropriate for a pond-side structure with wrought-iron strap hinges, latches, and door pulls. Cap the roof or cupola with a weathervane. Underscore the building's use as a potting shed by installing window boxes and trellises. Or make the shed a miniature version of your home, using the same materials, windows, and exterior stain or paint found in the "big house." In addition to these ideas, use the following Smart Steps to keep your outdoor area neat and organized.

Above: Paint a toy shed like a garden folly, blending fun colors with the garden.

Right: Integrate the shed into the surroundings. This one does double duty: storage and a destination on the garden path.

Above: Corral trash cans and recycling bins. A secure latch on the door helps to keep out raccoons.

Below: Hide trash behind ready-made fencing. If space requires you to keep trash near outdoor seating and dining, bag it securely and wash receptacles regularly.

SMART tip Trash to Treasure

Give an old, rigid metal rake a new life by attaching its head to a wall and hanging small gardening tools from its tines.

ONE Go weeding. And we're not talking crabgrass. Conduct an annual crusade to banish cracked planters; that shovel with a shattered handle; the hose that's more duct tape than PVC; bags and bottles with only a smidgen of their contents remaining. If you give these, and all the other defunct and defective outdoor-living items, the heave-ho, you'll have more room to keep the useful implements.

TWO Take care of equipment. Particularly in four-season climates, it's a wise idea to care for equipment before it's put away for the year. In late fall, after the last turn in the lawn and garden, clean and oil the mower blades following the manufacturer's recommendations to keep them in top shape during the off-season. Likewise, pads and cushions for lawn furniture should never be put away dirty: this is how mold happens. Drain all your hoses and sprinklers. Scrub grill grates and let them dry thoroughly, and cover or put the grill away for the winter. By being proactive, you'll be ready to roll on the first nice day of spring.

THREE Clear a path. While this is sound advice for any effective storage plan, because of the frequent back-and-forth nature of yard work and the many sharp cutting tools involved in it, it's especially important to try to keep items off the floor and out from underfoot. Around the pool, where a slip or fall could be quite hazardous, extra effort should be made to keep clutter in check.

Right: The serious gardeners ultimate dream: an entire shed assigned to hold tools and garden treasures awaiting placement.

CREATING ORDER

Whether custom constructed or ready-made, your new shed should be neat and well organized. Carefully plan the interior spaces to suit your needs. If the shed must meet several storage goals, section or zone the inside with one wall or area, perhaps, designated for sports gear and toys, another for garden and lawn care, and another for party or pool gear.

Add Helpers. Add appropriate storage helpers: bins, racks, and shelving hooks. Mount brackets on walls or ceilings to hold bikes and ladders; use large hooks for lawn chairs. Scour the hardware store and home center for any one of a number of tool towers to corral garden rakes, brooms, and shovels, keeping them off of the shed floor. The shed is another great spot for waterproof lightweight plastic storage boxes with built-in handles. These seal tightly, can be stacked if necessary, and are easy to carry around.

SMARTtip Heavenly Spot

It's possible to turn a standard multipurpose storage shed into a gardener's Eden by outfitting it with a sturdy potting bench, a utility sink, and lots of shelves for supplies. Orient windows for optimal sunlight; a skylight adds to the greenhouse effect.

SMARTtip Conceal Cans

Don't let garbage cans and recycling bins intrude on your landscape. Build a plywood locker to keep them out of sight (and out of reach of raccoons and other uninvited guests).

Prime Space. Store the most used items in the prime areas that are most accessible, usually near the front and low on shelves. Stash the infrequently used stuff on top shelves.

Keep Like Items Together. For instance, hang small garden tools together on a pegboard screwed or nailed to studs on a wall. Drill holes in garden tool handles so you can thread a leather or cord hanging loop. Garden tools can also be kept in a cart or a caddy made specifically for this purpose. Group sports gear by sport and then by season. Look for specially designed racks that combine baskets for balls and hooks for sticks, rackets, bats, and helmets.

SMALLER STORAGE NEEDS

If your storage needs don't warrant a full-fledged outbuilding, look to furnishings made of resin, teak, cedar, or mahogany—all of which can stand up to the elements—to keep the outdoor environment orderly. Wheels on benches, boxes, and tables let you rearrange the pieces to suit your needs.

Grill Supplies. Consider a separate plastic cabinet to stash grill supplies like barbecue tools, charcoal, and wood chips out of the weather.

Above: Smaller outdoor spaces demand storage creativity. Stash stuff out of sight, behind lattice.

Left: A grill-on-wheels offers a built-in cabinet for barbecue gear.

Opposite: Use the space under the deck steps to construct a cabinet for toys, tools, and sports gear. Do not store flammables here.

Under the Deck Area. Install weatherproof panels or lattice to the underneath area of an elevated deck to create dry, sheltered storage. Lay down interlocking concrete pavers, and you've got a covered patio where grills, bikes, and the like can be stowed out of the elements.

Trap Door. Cut a hatch or trap door into the floor of an on-grade wooden deck. Then build a box below the deck surface to provide a hideaway for barbecue tools, extra lawn chairs, hoses, and other items that can withstand bad weather.

In most yards, walls—those stalwarts of indoor storage—are in short supply. One spot that can be pressed into service is the backside of a fence. Use hooks and brackets to secure long, flat nets and skimmers for the pool; small implements like trowels, claws, and dibblers are kept convenient for the gardener.

Pool Equipment. Swimming pools come complete with their own unique set of accessories that need to be tucked away. If you don't have a cabana or pool house, keep floating lounges, noodles, and kickboards organized by slipping them into a freestanding rack. A poolside towel tree, with multiple swinging "branches," lets towels air-dry while keeping them tidy.

Because pool and yard equipment is exposed to lots of water in the course of their use, choose rust-resistant hooks and fasteners for storing items.

Pets, kids, and pool or lawn chemicals aren't compatible. Make sure any shed or cupboards can be locked.

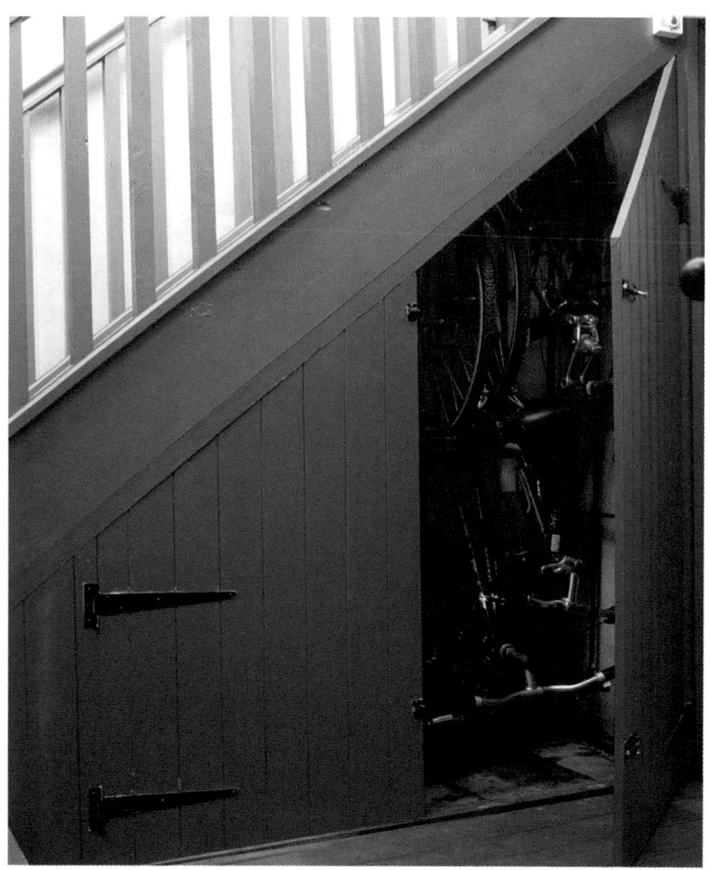

SMART tip — At the Ready

Store smoking chips and charcoal where they can be kept dry: in a canister and off the ground.

a gallery of...

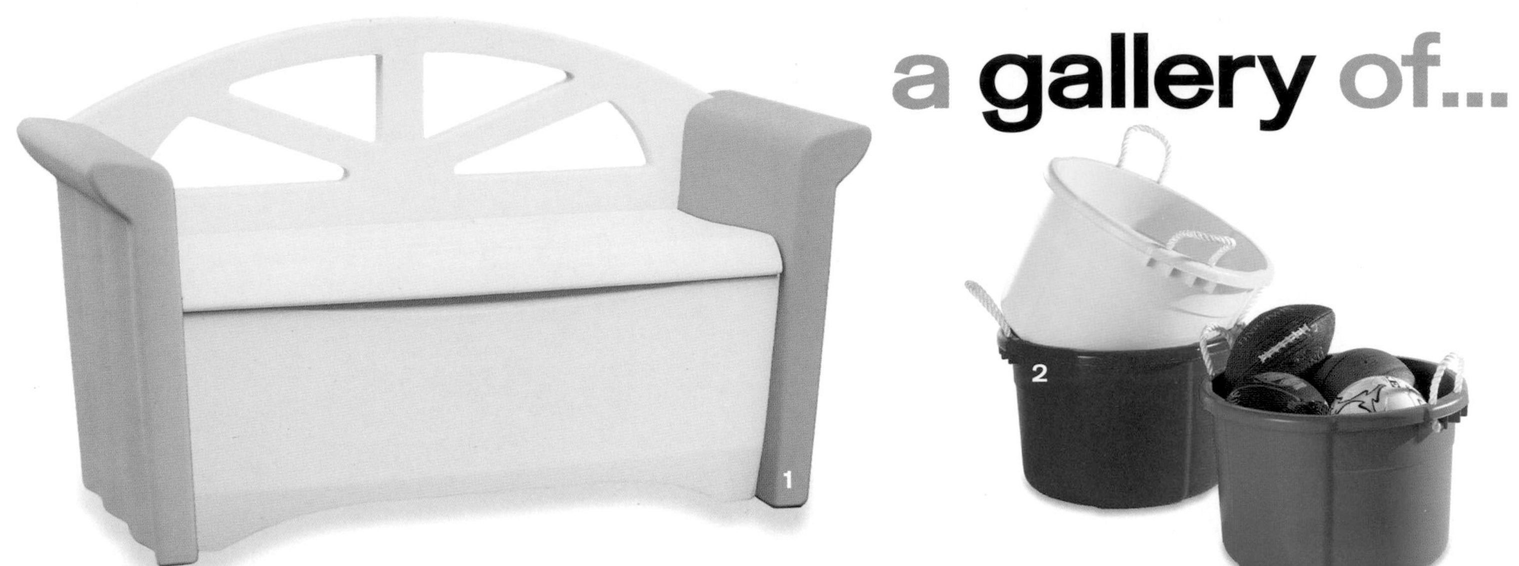

4

6

1 Look for benches that offer storage under the seat.

2 Keep the kids' play gear as accessible and as easy to put away as possible by using large, sturdy plastic bins.

3 Hinged sections of lattice under the deck hide storage for pool gear and other items you don't want on view.

4 Keep seeds in original packaging, and stash them in cubbies or in recycled small glass jars with screw-on lids.

5 Sturdy ready-mades withstand weather.

6 An outdoor kitchen provides lots of storage for barbecue and party gear.

7 A sink, workspace, and shelf storage for flower arranging and potting can be concealed behind folding doors.

...smart **ideas**

5

7

RESOURCE GUIDE

The following list of manufacturers and associations is meant to be a general guide to additional industry and product-related sources. It is not intended as a listing of products and manufacturers represented by the photographs in this book.

Acco Brands, Inc.
300 Tower Pkwy.
Lincolnshire, OH 60069
800-989-4923
www.acco.com
Manufactures office products.

Akro-Mils, a div. of Myers Industries
1293 S. Main St.
Akron, OH 44301
330-253-5592
www.akro-mils.com
Manufactures plastic storage products.

All Multimedia Storage
9706 NW Henry Ct.
Portland, OR 97229
866-603-1700
www.allmultimediastorage.com
Manufactures media storage.

Archival Methods
235 Middle Rd.
Henrietta, NY 14467
866-877-7050
www.archivalmethods.com
Manufactures storage products.

Bush Furniture
P.O. Box 460
1 Mason Dr.
Jamestown, NY 14702
716-665-2000
www.bushfurniture.com
Manufactures furniture.

California Closets
1000 Fourth St., Ste. 800
San Rafael, CA 94901
415-256-8501
www.californiaclosets.com
Manufactures closet systems.

Case Logic, Inc.
6303 Dry Creek Pkwy.
Longmont, CO 80503
800-447-4848
www.caselogic.com
Manufactures media storage.

Closet Maid
800-874-0008
www.closetmaid.com
Manufactures closet systems.

Columbia Storage Systems
3721 NW 16th St.
Camas, WA 98607
888-833-9190
www.columbiastoragesystems.com
Manufactures storage products.

Discgear
15505 Long Vista Dr.
Ste. 250
Austin, TX 78728
800-388-7597
www.discgear.com
Manufactures storage for CDs and portable CD players.

Easy Closets
20 Stonehouse Rd.
Millington, NJ 07946
800-910-0129
www.easyclosets.com
Manufactures closet systems.

Elfa
www.elfa.com
Manufactures storage products.

Ethan Allen
www.ethanallen.com
Manufactures furniture.

Fellowes, Inc.
1789 Norwood Ave.
Itasca, IL 60143
800-955-0959
www.fellowes.com
Manufactures paper shredders.

GarageWerks
P.O. Box 800
Ada, MI 49301
866-999-3757
www.garagewerks.com
Manufactures garage storage products.

Gautier
3155 N. Andrews Ave. Extension
Pompano Beach, FL 33064
954-975-3303
www.gautierusa.com
Manufactures furniture.

Gladiator GarageWorks, a div. of Whirlpool
www.gladiatorgw.com
Manufactures garage storage systems.

Hafele
www.hafeleonline.com
Manufactures cabinet hardware.

Ikea
www.ikea.com
Manufactures furniture and home-organization accessories.

Industrial House
800-650-5864
www.industrialhouse.com
Manufactures wire shelving units.

RESOURCE GUIDE

KidKraft
4630 Olin Rd.
Dallas, TX 75244
800-933-0771
www.kidkraft.com
Manufactures children's furniture.

Kraftmaid Cabinetry
P.O. Box 1055
15535 S. State Ave.
Middlefield, OH 44062
440-632-5333
www.kraftmaid.com
Manufactures cabinetry.

La-Z-Boy
www.la-z-boy.com
Manufactures furniture.

Manhattan Cabinetry
800-626-4288
www.manhattancabinetry.com
Manufactures Murphy beds.

Merillat
www.merillat.com
Manufactures cabinets.

ORG
www.home-org.com
Manufactures home-organization products.

O'Sullivan Furniture
www.osullivan.com
Manufactures furniture.

Plain & Fancy Custom Cabinetry
Oak St. and Rte. 501
Schaefferstown, PA 17088
800-447-9006
www.plainfancycabinetry.com
Manufactures custom cabinetry.

Polder
www.polder.com
Manufactures home-organization products.

The Preservation Station
12308 Mulberry Ct.
Woodbridge, VA 22192
571-344-1453
www.preservesmart.com
Manufactures acid-free tissue paper and materials for garment preservation.

Robern, a div. of Kohler
www.robern.com
Manufactures medicine cabinets.

Rubbermaid
3320 W. Market St.
Fairlawn, OH 44333
888-895-2110
www.rubbermaid.com
Manufactures home-storage products.

Sauder
800-523-3987
www.sauder.com
Manufactures furniture.

Schulte
12115 Ellington Ct.
Cincinnati, OH 45249
800-669-3225
www.shultestorage.com
Manufactures storage systems and accessories.

Sharp USA
www.sharpusa.com
Manufactures consumer electronics.

Sony USA
www.sony.com
Manufactures consumer electronics.

Spinkeeper
www.spinkeeper.com
Manufactures CD and DVD organizers.

Stacks and Stacks
1045 Hensley St.
Richmond, CA 94801
800-761-5222
www.stacksandstacks.com
Manufactures storage and organization products.

Stickley Furniture
1 Stickley Dr.
P.O. Box 480
Manlius, NY 13104
315-682-5500
www.stickley.com
Manufactures furniture.

Storic
12400 Hwy. 71 W.
Ste. 350-172
Austin, TX 78738
800-672-4954
www.storic.com
Manufactures storage products.

Studio RTA
7255 Rosemead Blvd.
Pico Rivero, CA 90660
562-446-2255
www.studiorta.com
Manufactures ready-to-assemble furniture.

White Home Products
400 N. 14th St.
Kenilworth, NJ 07033
800-896-0902
www.closets.net
Manufactures the Closet Carousel.

GLOSSARY

Accent Lighting: A type of lighting that highlights an area or object to emphasize that aspect of a room's character.

Ambient Lighting: General illumination that surrounds a room. The light's source is not visible.

Appliance Garage: A small cabinet intended for housing a small appliance, such as a standing mixer. It is mounted on the countertop below the wall units and typically features a roll-up (tambour) or top-hinged door. Appliance garages keep the work surface unobstructed.

Armoire: A solid cabinet, usually made of wood, that holds entertainment equipment or clothing.

Backlighting: Illumination coming from a source behind or at the side of an object.

Backsplash: The vertical section at the rear and sides of a countertop that protects the adjacent wall.

Base Cabinet: A cabinet that rests on the floor under a countertop or vanity.

Built-In: Any element, such as a bookcase or cabinet, that is built into a wall or an existing frame.

Carousel Shelves: Shelves that attach to the backs of two right-angled doors and rotate 270 degrees.

Case Goods: Furniture that is used for storage, such as cabinets, dressers, and desks.

Clearance: The amount of space between two fixtures, the centerlines of two fixtures, or a fixture and an obstacle, such as a wall or a large piece of furniture.

Code: A locally or nationally enforced mandate regarding structural design, materials, plumbing, or electrical systems that state what you can or cannot do when building or remodeling.

Contemporary: Any modern design (after 1920) that does not contain traditional elements.

Dimmer Switch: A switch that can vary the intensity of the light it controls.

Distressed Finish: A decorative paint technique in which the final paint coat is sanded and battered to produce the markings of wear and the patina of age.

Dovetail: A joinery method in which wedge-shaped parts are interlocked to form a tight bond. This joint is commonly used in furniture making.

Dowel: A short cylinder, made of wood, metal, or plastic, that fits into corresponding holes bored in two pieces of wood, creating a joint.

Faux Finish: A decorative paint technique that imitates a pattern found in nature.

Flat-Screen TV: A TV with a flat display.

Focal Point: The dominant element in a room or design, usually the first to catch your eye.

Fold-Down Shelf: A spring-loaded shelf that swings up and out of a base cabinet for use, then folds down and back into the cabinet when it's not needed.

Framed Cabinet: A cabinet with a full frame across the face of the cabinet box.

Frameless Cabinet: A cabinet without a face frame. It may also be called a "European-style" cabinet.

Hardware: Wood, plastic, or metal-plated trim found on the exterior of furniture, such as knobs, handles, and decorative trim.

Lazy Susan: A shelf that rotates 360 degrees.

Modular: Units of a standard size, such as pieces of a cabinet or wall system, that can be fitted together.

Molding: An architectural band used to trim a line where materials join or to create a linear decoration. It is typically made of wood, plaster, or a polymer.

Mortise-and-Tenon Joinery: A joint in which a hole (mortise) is cut into one piece of wood to receive a projecting piece (tenon) cut into another.

Murphy Bed: A bed that folds into the wall or a closet when not in use.

Occasional Piece: A small piece of furniture for incidental use, such as an end table.

Orientation: The placement of any object or space, such as a window, a door, or a room, and its relationship to the points on a compass.

Panel: A flat, rectangular piece of material that forms part of a wall, door, or cabinet. Typically made of wood, it is usually framed by a border and either raised or recessed.

Proportion: The relationship of one object to another.

Pullout: A full-extension cabinet component, such as a built-in pantry, hamper, basket, or shelf that is fitted with ball-bearing slides for ease of operation.

Scale: The size of a room or object.

Sight Line: The natural line of sight the eye travels when looking into or around a room.

Slide-Out: See "Pullout."

Soffit: A boxed-in area just below the ceiling and above a cabinet.

Space Configuration: A design term that is used to describe the reallocation of interior space without adding on.

Stud: A vertical support element made of wood or metal that is used in the construction of walls.

Surround: The enclosure and area around a tub or shower.

Task Lighting: Lighting that is concentrated in specific areas for tasks such as preparing food, applying makeup, reading, or doing crafts.

Tilt-Down Tray: The hinged, flat panel in front of the sink that tilts down to reveal a small storage pocket.

Tongue-and-Groove Joinery: A joinery technique in which a protruding end (tongue) fits into a recess (groove), locking the two pieces together.

Track Lighting: Lighting that utilizes a fixed band to carry electrical current and hold movable light fixtures.

Uplight: Also used to describe the lights themselves, this is actually the term for light that is directed upward toward the ceiling.

Veneer: High-quality wood that is cut into very thin sheets for use as a surface material.

Vintage: Anything that is at least 20-25 years old, but not antique (at least 100 years old).

INDEX

PHOTO CREDITS

page 1: Sam Gray **page 5:** Mark Lohman **page 8:** www.alanshortall.com **page 9:** *left* www.alanshortall.com; *right* Mark Lohman **page 10:** Mark Lohman **page 12:** Jessie Walker **page 13:** *top* Jessie Walker; *center* Tony Giammarino/Giammarino & Dworkin, design: Christine McCabe; *bottom* Bob Greenspan, stylist: Susan Andrews **page 14:** *top* Mark Samu; *bottom* Roy Inman, stylist: Susan Andrews **page 15:** *top left* Tony Giammarino/Giammarino & Dworkin, design: Bruce Bierman Design; *top right* Tria Giovan; *bottom* Jessie Walker **page 16:** www.alanshortall.com **page 17:** *top* Ken Gutmaker; *bottom* Mark Lohman **page 18:** *top* Jessie Walker; *bottom* Mark Lohman, design: Dan Marty **page 19:** Mark Lohman **page 20:** Tria Giovan **page 21:** Ken Gutmaker **page 22:** Tony Giammarino/Giammarino & Dworkin, design: Christine McCabe **page 23:** *top* www.davidduncanlivingston.com; *center* Todd Caverly/Brian Vanden Brink photos, builder: Mark Wild; *bottom* Ken Gutmaker **page 24:** George Ross/CH **page 25:** *top* Sam Gray, design: Bierly-Drake, Inc.; *bottom* George Ross/CH **page 26:** *top* Tria Giovan; *bottom* Tony Giammarino/Giammarino & Dworkin, design: Christine McCabe **page 27:** *left* Nancy Elizabeth Hill, design: Karen Houghton Interiors; *right* Eric Roth, design: Van Millwork and Benjamin Moore Paints **page 28:** Todd Caverly/Brian Vanden Brink photos, builder: Mark Wild **page 29:** *top* Jessie Walker, architect: Dave McFadden; *bottom* Nancy Elizabeth Hill, design: Diane Burgoyne Interiors **page 30:** *top* Nancy Elizabeth Hill, architect: Huestis Tucker Architects; *bottom* Eric Roth, architect: Warren Cunningham Architects **page 31:** Bob Greenspan, stylist: Susan Andrews **page 32-35:** *all* www.alanshortall.com **page 36:** *top* Tony Giammarino/Giammarino & Dworkin, design: Marge Thomas; *bottom* Mark Samu, design: Jean Stoffer Designs, Ltd. **page 37:** courtesy of Kraftmaid Cabinetry **page 38:** Eric Roth, design: Dalia Kitchen Design **page 39:** Mark Samu, design: Kitchens by Ken Kelly **page 40:** *both* courtesy of Plain & Fancy Custom Cabinetry **page 41:** *top left* Eric Roth, design: Dalia Kitchen Design; *bottom left* Eric Roth, design: Dalia Kitchen Design; *right* Mark Samu, design: Jean Stoffer Designs, Ltd. **page 42:** *left* Mark Samu, design: Jean Stoffer Designs, Ltd.; *top right* Eric Roth, design: Dalia Kitchen Design; *center right* Eric Roth, architect: Feinman Inc. Architects; *bottom right* Mark Samu, design: Kitchens by Ken Kelly **page 43:** Mark Samu, design: Jean Stoffer Designs, Ltd. **page 44-45:** *all* courtesy of Plain & Fancy Custom Cabinetry **page 46-47:** Mark Samu, design: Kitchen Dimensions **page 48:** Mark Samu, design: Jean Stoffer Designs, Ltd. **page 49:** Eric Roth, architect: Catalano Architects **page 50:** K. Rice/H. Armstrong Roberts **page 51:** *top* Tony Giammarino/Giammarino & Dworkin; *center* Mark Lohman, design: S. Philipp Design; *bottom* Mark Lohman, architect: Doug Burdge Associates **page 52-53:** *all* Mark Lohman, architect: Doug Burdge Associates **page 55:** www.davidduncanlivingston.com **page 56:** Nancy Elizabeth Hill, design: Rooms of England by Pamela **page 57:** *top* Mark Lohman, design: Janet Lohman; *bottom left* K. Rice/H. Armstrong Roberts; *bottom right* Brian Vanden Brink, architect: Pete Bethanis **page 58:** *both* Ken Gutmaker **page 59:** *top* Mark Lohman, architect:

Doug Burdge Associates; *bottom* Tria Giovan **page 60:** Mark Lohman **page 61:** *top left* Mark Lohman; *top right* Mark Lohman, design: William Hefner Architects; *bottom left* Tony Giammarino/Giammarino & Dworkin; *bottom right* Mark Lohman, design: Janet Lohman **page 63:** *both* Mark Lohman, design: S. Philipp Design **page 64:** *top* Mark Lohman, design: Janet Lohman; *bottom* Mark Lohman, architect: Doug Burdge Associates **page 65:** *top* Tony Giammarino/Giammarino & Dworkin *bottom* Mark Lohman **page 66:** Mark Lohman, design: Janet Lohman **page 67:** Brian Vanden Brink **page 68:** *top left* Jessie Walker, architect: Paul Konstant; *top right* Tria Giovan; *bottom left* Jessie Walker, architect: Paul Konstant; *bottom right* Mark Lohman, architect: William Hefner Architects **page 69:** *all* Mark Lohman **page 70:** Mark Samu, design: Sherill Canet Design **page 71:** *top* Ken Gutmaker; *center* Mark Lohman; *bottom* Brian Vanden Brink **page 72:** Mark Lohman, design: Debra Jones **page 73-75:** www.alanshortall.com **page 76:** *top* Bob Greenspan, stylist: Susan Andrews; *bottom* Ken Gutmaker **page 77:** *both* Nancy Elizabeth Hill, design: Kitchens by Deane **page 78:** George Ross/CH **page 80:** *top* Mark Lohman, design: Dan Berman; *bottom* George Ross/CH **page 80-81:** *left* www.alanshortall.com; *center* Brian Vanden Brink, architect: Sally Weston; *right* Mark Lohman, design: Harry Topping **page 82:** George Ross/CH **page 83:** *top* Brian Vanden Brink; *bottom* Bob Greenspan, stylist: Susan Andrews **page 84:** Mark Lohman, design: Barclay Butera, Inc. **page 85:** *top* courtesy of IKEA; *center* Brian Vanden Brink; *bottom* courtesy of California Closets **page 86-87:** *left* Brian Vanden Brink, architect: Julie Snow Architects; *center* Mark Lohman, design: Janet Lohman; *right* Brian Vanden Brink, architect: Polhemus Savery DaSilva Architects **page 88:** Brian Vanden Brink, architect: Whitten Winkleman Architects **page 89:** *top left & top right* courtesy of Manhattan Cabinetry; *bottom* courtesy of IKEA **page 90:** *top* IKEA; *bottom* Mark Samu courtesy of Hearst Magazines **page 91:** *top* Mark Lohman; *bottom* www.davidduncanlivingston.com **page 93:** *top* Brian Vanden Brink; *bottom* www.alanshortall.com **page 94-95:** *all* Tony Giammarino/Giammarino & Dworkin, design: Maureen Klein **page 96-97:** *left* courtesy of California Closets; *center* Brian Vanden Brink; *left* Abode Picture Library/Alamy **page 98:** *left* Mark Samu; *right* www.alanshortall.com **page 99:** courtesy of Closetmaid **page 100:** Eric Roth, closet: Kathleen Sullivan Elliot **page 101:** www.alanshortall.com **page 102:** courtesy of IKEA **page 103:** www.carolynbates.com **page 104:** *top left & top right* Brian Vanden Brink, architect: Scholz & Barclay Architecture; *bottom left* www.alanshortall.com; *bottom right* Eric Roth **page 105:** *top* Mark Samu, design: Lee Najman Design; *bottom left & bottom right* Mark Lohman **page 106:** *top left* Mark Lohman, design: Sean Taddey; *top right* Brian Vanden Brink, architect: Peter Rose Architects; *bottom* courtesy of ORG **page 107:** *top left* Mark Samu, design: KJS Interiors; *top right* courtesy of IKEA; *bottom* courtesy of California Closets **page 108:** Brian Vanden Brink, architect: Sally Weston **page 109:** *top* Brian Vanden Brink, architect: Sally Weston; *center* Jessie Walker; *bottom* Tony Giammarino/Giammarino & Dworkin, architect/builder: Steve Berg **page 110:** Mark Lohman Photography, design: Janet Lohman **page 111:** Tony Giammarino/Giammarino & Dworkin, architect/builder: Steve Berg **page 112:** Bob Greenspan, stylist: Susan Andrews **page 113:** *top & center* courtesy of Kraftmaid Cabinetry, *bottom* courtesy of Merillat **page 114:** *top* Brian Vanden Brink, architect: Sally Weston; *bottom* Brian Vanden Brink, architect: Elliott Elliott Norelius Architects **page 115:** *top* Winifried Heinze/Redcover.com; *bottom* Mark Samu **page 116:** *left* Nancy Elizabeth Hill/Stirling Design Associates; *left* Mark Samu, architect: Sam Scofield AIA **page 117:** *top* Tria Giovan; *bottom* Mark Lohman, design: Kathryne Designs **page 118:** *top* Mark Lohman, architect: William Hefner Architects; *bottom* Tria Giovan **page 119:** Nancy Elizabeth Hill **page 120:** Mark Samu, builder: John Hummel Builder, design: Ruth Sommers Design **page 121:** *top left* Jessie Walker; *top right & center* Tria Giovan; *bottom left* Roy Inman, stylist: Susan Andrews; *bottom right* Mark Lohman **page 122:** *top left* courtesy of Kraftmaid Cabinetry; *top right* courtesy of Closetmaid; *bottom left* Tony Giammarino/Giammarino & Dworkin, architect/builder: Steve Berg; *bottom right* courtesy of Merillat **page 123:** *top* courtesy of Merillat *bottom left* Jessie Walker *bottom right* courtesy of Polder **page 124:** courtesy of Kraftmaid Cabinetry **page 125:** *top* Brian Vanden Brink, design: Custom Electronics; *center* courtesy of IKEA; *bottom* Ken Hayden/Redcover.com **page 126:** courtesy of Kraftmaid Cabinetry **page 127:** Phillip H. Ennis, design: Greenbaum Interiors/Lynn Cone, architect: Moisan Architects **page 128-129:** *left* courtesy of La-Z-Boy; *center* Mark York/Redcover.com; *top right* courtesy of Stickley Furniture; *bottom right* courtesy of Kraftmaid Cabinetry **page 130-131:** *left & center* Mark Lohman; *right* Mark Samu; **page 132-133:** Mark Lohman **page 134:** www.alanshortall.com **page 135:** Bob Greenspan, stylist: Susan Andrews **page 136:** *top* courtesy of Sharp USA; *bottom left* courtesy of Sony; *bottom right* Mark Lohman **page 137:** *both* Brian Vanden Brink, design: Custom Electronics **page 138:** Roger Turk Northlight Photography, architect: Drager/Gould Architects **page 139:** *top* Brian Vanden Brink, architect: Centerbrook Architects; *center* Ken Hayden/Redcover.com, design: Michael Reeves *bottom* www.carolynbates.com, architect: Ted Montgomery/Groundswell Archiects **page 140:** *top* Mark Lohman, design: Barclay Butera, Inc. *bottom* Mark Lohman **page 141:** *top* Arcaid/Alamy *bottom* Abode Interiors Picture Library / Alamy **page 142:** www.davidduncanlivingston.com **page 143:** *top* Henry Wilson/Redcover.com, architects: Ian Chee & Voon Yee Wong for VW Architects, design: Florence Lim; *bottom* Brian Vanden Brink, architect: Centerbrook Architects **page 144:** Mark Samu, builder: Amedore Homes **page 145:** *top* Johnny Bouchier/Red cover.com *bottom* Elizabeth Whiting & Associates/Alamy **page 146:** *top* Mark Samu *bottom* www.davidduncanlivingston.com **page 147:** *top* Mark Lohman, design: Darren Hinault Interior Design *bottom* Tria Giovan **page 148:** *top left* Eric Roth, design: Kathleen Sullivan Elliott; *top center* NDisc/Alamy; *top right* Mark Samu, builder: John Hummel Builder, design: Ruth Sommers Design; *bottom* Arcaid/Alamy **page 149:** Roger Turk Northlight Photography, architect: Chesmore/Buck Architects **page 150–151:** Ken Hayden/Redcover.com, design: Michael Reeves **page 152:** www.carolynbates.com, architect: Ted Montgomery/Groundswell Archiects **page 153:** *top* Abode Interiors Picture Library / Alamy; *bottom* Paul Massey/Redcover.com **page 154:** *left* Brian Vanden Brink; *right* Roger Turk Northlight Photography, design: Masterplan Remodeling **page 155:** *top* Roger Turk, Northlight Photography; *bottom left* www.davidduncanlivingston.com; *bottom right* Bob Greenspan, stylist: Susan Andrews **page 156:** Mark Lohman Photography **page 157:** *top left & top right* Tria Giovan; *bottom left* www.davidduncanlivingston.com; *bottom right* Brian Vanden Brink, architect: Stephen Blatt Architects **page 158:** Niall McDiarmid/Redcover.com **page 159:** *top* Johnny Bouchier/Redcover.com; *center & bottom* www.alanshortall.com **page 160:** *top left* www.alanshortall.com; *top right* courtesy of Rubbermaid; *bottom* www.alanshortall.com **page 161:** *top* courtesy of Rubbermaid **page 162:** *top* Guglielmo Galvin/Redcover.com; *bottom left* courtesy of Rubbermaid; *bottom right* Johnny Bouchier/Redcover.com; **page 163:** *both* www.alanshortall.com **page 164:** www.davidduncanlivingston.com **page 166:** Brian Vanden Brink, architect: Whitten Winkleman Architects **page 167:** Tria Giovan **page 168:** Abode Interiors Picture Library/Alamy **page 169:** *top* Verity Welstead/Redcover.com; *bottom* Winifried Heinz/Redcover.com **page 170-171:** *left* Roy Inman, stylist: Susan Andrews; *top* Bob Greenspan, stylist: Susan Andrews; *bottom* Jessie Walker **page 172:** Tony Giammarino/Giammarino & Dworkin, design: Christine McCabe **page 173:** Jessie Walker, design: Christine Baumbach **page 174:** courtesy of Whirlpool **page 175:** *top* Jessie Walker; *bottom* Jessie Walker, architect: John Myefski of Wickets Fine Cabinetry **page 176:** *left* Brian Vanden Brink, architect: Whitten Winkleman Architects; *right* Tria Giovan **page 177:** *top left* Huntley Hedworth/Redcover.com; *top right* Johnny Bouchier/Redcover.com; *bottom left* courtesy of Rubbermaid; *bottom right* Eric Roth, architect: David Pill Architects **page 178:** Mark Lohman **page 179:** *top* Tony Giammarino/Giammarino & Dworkin ; *center* Mark Samu; *bottom* Jessie Walker **page 180:** Bradley Olman **page 181:** *top* courtesy of Whirlpool; *bottom* Tim Evan-Cook/Red-cover.com **page 182:** Mark Lohman, design: Kitty Bartholomew **page 183:** *top* Jessie Walker, design: Lydia Grabemann of LSG Interiors; *center* Tony Giammarino/Giammarino & Dworkin; *bottom* Bradley Olman **page 184:** courtesy of ORG **page 185:** *top* courtesy of ORG; *bottom* Index Open **page 186:** *top left* Tony Giammarino/Giammarino & Dworkin; *top right* Bradley Olman; *bottom left* Jessie Walker, design: Lydia Grabemann of LSG Interiors; *bottom right* Tony Giammarino/Giammarino & Dworkin **page 187:** *top* Tony Giammarino/Giammarino & Dworkin; *bottom* Nancy Elizabeth Hill, design: Karen Houghton Interiors **page 188:** Natalie Charles/Merrist Wood College, design: Photos Horticultural **page 189:** *top* Brian Vanden Brink, architect: Carol Wilson; *center* Brad Simmons, stylist: ShelterStyle.com; *bottom* courtesy of Rubbermaid **page 190:** *top* Hugh Palmer/Redcover.com *bottom* Ed Reeve/Redcover.com **page 191:** *top* Ed Reeve/Redcover.com ; *bottom* John Glover, design: Alan Titchmarsh **page 192:** *top* Jessie Walker; *bottom* Photos Horticultural **page 193:** Brad Simmons, stylist: ShelterStyle.com **page 194-195:** *left* courtesy of Wolf/Subzero; *center* Crandall & Crandall; *right* Amanda Turner/Redcover.com; **page 196:** *top* courtesy of Rubbermaid; *bottom* courtesy of National Pool & Spa Institute **page 197:** *top left* Johnny Bouchier/Redcover.com; *top right* Lee Photographers/Ken Graber; *bottom left* courtesy of Rubbermaid; *bottom right* Brian Vanden Brink, architect: Carol Wilson

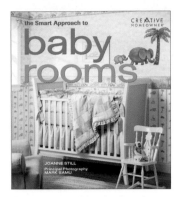

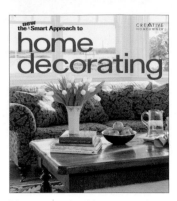

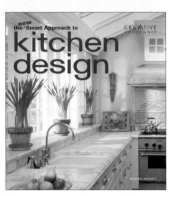

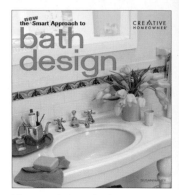

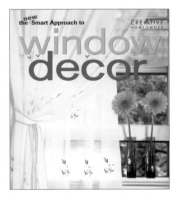

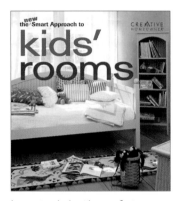

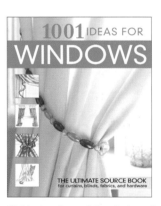

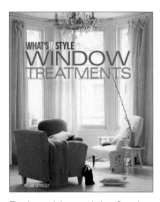

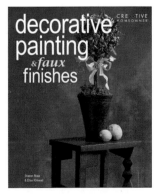

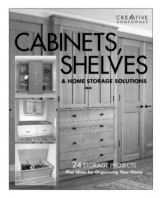

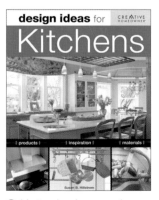